THE GATEKEEPER

What God Created the Man to Be

Dr. Jerry Tallo

ISBN 978-1-63961-152-2 (paperback)
ISBN 978-1-63961-153-9 (digital)

Christian Faith Publishing, Inc.
832 Park Avenue
Meadville, PA 16335
www.christianfaithpublishing.com

Printed in the United States of America

Endorsement

This is a timely and absolutely vital book! Jerry Tallo speaks into the heart of Biblical maleness, cutting through the cultural darkness like a lighthouse shining across a storm-tossed sea.

When it comes to men and their families, he gives us "an arial view of the man as the gatekeeper." Find out what this means and, more importantly, how to be one. Jerry writes from a depth of life experience, which I have been blessed to observe personally.

Using sound theological language, he builds an accurate Kingdom framework to guide any serious Christ-follower toward a redemptive pathway of manhood, constantly reminding us that "we have Jesus to make us great gatekeepers."

If the theological rubber ever meets the practical road, you can read it here, then put these truths to action!

Dr. Clem Ferris, Elder
Grace Church, Chapel Hill, NC
Itinerant Teaching and Prophetic Ministry
Author and Church Consultant

Contents

Introduction 7

Part 1: Worldview and Man's Role as Gatekeeper

1 Worldview 13
2 Covenant—The Worldview by Which We
   Should Live 28
3 A Man, His Family, and the Covenant Model 40
4 Representation—A Secret Weapon 52
5 Origins—Who God Really Created the Man to Be 62
6 The Man's Big Problem from the Fall 77
7 The Man as Gatekeeper—A Picture Painted 95

Part 2: Let's Man Up to the Doctrines, Principles, and
Threats That Determine My Success as the Gatekeeper

8 Depravity 109
9 The Unreconciled Conscience 116
10 The Awareness Meter 122
11 Passivity 125
12 Adolescence and Coddling 131
13 Repentance 137
14 Thinking Like a Gatekeeper 140

Some Highly Recommended Books 143

Introduction

I grew up in an Italian Catholic family in Upstate New York, the oldest of three boys. Dad and Mom were tough but sacrificed what little they had to make their sons successful. My brothers and I will always be grateful.

For some reason, I got into my share of trouble with the nuns at St. Rita's School (grades 1 to 8) in Webster, New York. Trouble and fights seemed to find me. I once went to my dad and advised him of the unusual names a couple guys were calling me, having to do with my Italian descent. Dad looked at me with that fire in his eyes and simply said, "Son, the next time one of them calls you that, pop him in the jaw."

That was the launch of my amateur on-the-street pugilistic adventures. Never once do I recall Dad feeling sorry for me or my brothers if we ended up on the losing side. I also never remember him bailing on us; rather, he and Mom showed us how to work through adversity and lack without whining.

Little did I realize we were being groomed to deal with the routine pressures of life as men. Though Dad was not an educated man, he taught us through his dogged simplicity, while Mom inspired us to outthink our competition. My brothers Lou and Mark are great men who have done much for their families and our society.

Fast-forward to December 12, 1979, when Jesus reached into my depraved soul and gave me eternal life. By His grace, I've never looked back and was always drawn to deeper learning of the Holy Scriptures. I heard Bible teachers postulating a peaceful, quiet gospel, in which men behaved nicely at all times. While much of it spoke to my soul, something was disconnected.

Then, in 1985, the males in their teens and early twenties were flocking to the theaters to see a film called *Rambo: First Blood Part II*. So my buddy and I went to see it to determine what in it called to young men.

Well, I couldn't get enough of it and didn't want it to end (probably to the chagrin of some Bible teachers). So I took the only logical action later that week—I rented *First Blood*, Stallone's first film about the tragic reluctant war hero John Rambo.

Those films had reawakened the warrior in me, and the Lord mercifully directed me to channel that into becoming the "gatekeeper" to my family. Jesus is both the Mighty Warrior and Prince of Peace, and His Spirit is within us to live in a holy balance of both. We need to see it happen.

This book is the fruit of such a journey with my wife, five sons, and three daughters. I wouldn't trade those years for anything.

So here is why I wrote it:

- God created a man to be a gatekeeper—it's who man is inside, and that needs to be released.
- Men need to get hold of this profound but simple calling and let it awaken their noble souls.
- The family is still God's key to the health of any nation; the family needs a real gatekeeper.
- Our culture now resists strong men, which is too bad, because it's who we are.
- This book will inspire you to get there.

This book is not an attack against belief systems or cultural trends that don't line up with the Scriptures. It is not a call away from modernism's norms but rather a call to a time-honored view of the man as keeper of his gate. If you're looking for a fight, for something to criticize or vilify because a biblical look at manhood is offensive or "outdated" to you, then don't read it. I'm not after a cause.

If you want an objective analysis of who and what the male is created by God to be and function as on this earth, then this book is for you. It is geared toward

- men who want to discover who they are
- men who want to become who they are
- men who want to transform the next generation
- women who want their men to be the spiritual leader in the home
- women who need to know what to look for in a "biblical" husband
- parents who want their sons to have a healthy and strong family
- grandparents who want the same
- pastors and leaders who want their men transformed
- anyone who wants nobility restored to society

If you're willing to honestly challenge your old opinions, biases, and emasculated worldview, this book will

Provoke	Reveal	Renew your thinking
Instruct	Equip	Strengthen your backbone
Clarify	Inspire	Put you on your knees before Jesus

PART 1

Worldview and Man's Role as Gatekeeper

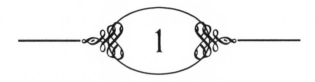

Worldview

What's All the Noise about Worldview?

When I stop at the grocery store and forget to buy eggs, we have no eggs in the house. If I spend all my money before the end of the month, I will have no money with which to pay my bills. If I walk out to the shed to get that bag of grass seed and the bag is empty, I have no grass seed. In each instance, I either did or did not have the object cited. I either got a base hit in yesterday's game, or I went without a hit. And so on...

However, this is not how a worldview works. I never "don't have it"—that's right, the two negatives give us a positive. I always have a worldview even if I don't know what it is. In fact, the fact that I don't know my worldview actually explains part of my worldview. Get it?

The point is that most of us don't know our own worldviews because we don't know what one is and how critically important it is to have a good one (whatever a good one is). Yet my ignorance never means I *don't have* a worldview by which I live.

So here is the bottom line about a worldview: You go to bed with it. You wake up with it. You go to work or school or practice or partying with it. You eat dinner with it. *It* never goes away. So it must be important, eh?

Let's try and make some sense of this.

What Is a Worldview?

The formal answer is this: A worldview is the set of beliefs and presuppositions I hold about the core realities of life that determine how I perceive, analyze, and respond to life as it happens around me and how I do *or do not* take action to impact that life.

The informal answer is this: A worldview is what I believe and why and how it affects the way I live life.

Sandy and I have been blessed with eight children: three daughters and five sons. Next to Jesus, my family is *it* to me, so my priority was always to invest in them—body, mind, and soul—to prepare them for life, with Jesus at the center.

We named our youngest daughter Maria after my maternal grandmother, a kind, quiet, sensitive soul. Well, God gave us that Maria from *The Sound of Music*—you know, the loud, mischievous adventurer. Our Maria is truly something special; she is fearlessly aggressive yet with a healthy self-awareness. When she enters a room, it changes.

She has no problem challenging her dad, mom, older siblings, her husband Colby (a true gift to our family), or anyone else who needs it. So a while back she and I were in a tough conversation about a worldview issue, and Maria asked me, "Why, Dad?"

I didn't like being put on the spot, so I pulled the Dad card and said, "What do you mean *why*?" Maria stared me down and simply replied, "Because you taught me to ask why. So why?" Ouch. Game, set, match. The student was the teacher at that moment. While I didn't like it, I was proud of her, because she was going to the root of the matter.

Friends, we cannot get to our worldview without the "why" asked and answered. "Why?" drove Aristotle, Alexander, and Nero; it drove the apostle Paul, Polycarp, and Martin Luther. George Washington, Robert E. Lee, and Thomas Edison asked "Why?" and "Why?" also bothered Hitler, Stalin, and Castro…the good guys and the bad ones.

Now, today's typical soul, being herded through life, has a simple answer for "Why?" He says, "I don't know," "It's cool," "Look at all the injustices in life," or my personal favorite, "Because."

"What" and "How" are much easier to process and answer, but the guy who says "Dunno" to why something happened has just given you his worldview: "Life happens and as long as it doesn't mess with me, who cares?" He doesn't know that he's on Earth because he has a destiny to impact others and to hopefully have answers that solve problems people cannot solve themselves. Nope, he's here to live life as it comes, get what he can out of it, make the best of things, and then whatever comes after this, so be it. As long as people leave him alone to do his thing, he's cool with life.

I brainwashed all my children from infancy—I even spoke to them regularly in the womb—that they were on the Earth to lead, not follow, and to be influencers, not *influencees* (new made-up word here). My worldview prompted and inspired me to inspire them. At the core of my life's message as a pastor and preacher for over three decades has been the call to think and live multigenerationally. This is a call from God we cannot escape, unless we ignore the call. This is a big "why" issue. I didn't just think it was a good idea. I needed a solid and valid reason. My worldview drives this viewpoint, because it carries a reason for the action, an answer to "why." It took time and effort to develop and clarify this view so it could be lived out.

The formal definition above speaks of my "presuppositions"—that which I take for granted in advance of the day's events, because of life's origins, and the causes of those things and events as I understand them to be. These presuppositions form a filter through which I see life around me. This filter results in my worldview—why stuff happens based upon what I believe and how I respond to it, or don't respond…which is still a response.

Here's a basic presupposition I hold: God has ordained my family name; therefore, those of us who carry it always represent it and are here to bring honor to it and the generations that came before us. Two of my boys, Bear and Trevor, each has the family name tattooed on his bicep. In fact, they got so original that they chose the name my paternal grandfather carried all his life, Taglienti, until an immigration agent at Ellis Island shortened it. I'm proud of my sons "carrying" the family name. The only problem having it on the bicep is if they quit working out and their arms sag like Jell-O, the name won't look right!

It's not complicated, but as we now see, it's critical to know our worldviews and if they line up with the Holy Scriptures. We'll get to this later.

While the infamous Karl Marx and I have rather contrary worldviews, we hold a major presupposition in common: we are on the Earth "to matter" for others. This demands living beyond my own comfort. Of course our commonality ends there. Just read the *Communist Manifesto* and you'll get Marx's worldview. Our job as men is to be able to answer questions like "Why such harsh contrarianism and violence are promoted by men like Marx?" and "Why do so many young people gravitate toward such teachings?" This understanding is important today because today's typical western young person's worldview is rooted in Marx even though they don't know it.

One more thought on the importance of forming a worldview: there are no vacuums in life. If I'm passive as a husband and/or father, someone else will fill the gap, and that could be a neighbor, relative, coach, teacher, guidance counselor, guru, etc. Thanks to the escapism of so many men today, most people have grown their worldviews by default through the influence, oppression, mental manipulation, or brainwashing by society's "experts" who are usually self-proclaimed.

Sadly, so many college graduates are default Marxists who want to overthrow established authority in the name of equality, but they cannot answer the "why" question in a truly objective analysis of their own viewpoint. For example, when questioned about what the source of revenues would be if all wages were equal for all vocations and if all college tuition were free, they have no answer. It's because the "why" has not been addressed.

Our middle daughter, Luissa, is a philosophical thinker like her dad. So when she was old enough to reason and drink coffee, one of my favorite times of day was morning joe with my daughter. We discussed news events, social issues and controversies, family dynamics and conflicts, behavioral patterns in her circles of friendship, and even the good and/or tragic happenings around us.

I witnessed her desire to understand the "why" behind life's journey, and to the best of my ability, I would interject biblical principles into the conversation and explain how the scriptures provided the best lens through which to see and understand life. We'd look at biblical origins and first principles, events, and outcomes in bible history and then super-impose the concept to modern-day realities.

It wasn't a complicated search to unlock "secret codes" in Scripture. Rather, we found relevant sections of Old or New Testament life that could correlate to the issue or problem at hand. We assumed that Scripture spoke to all of life, not just the spiritual realm.

Now I have this with her and my son-in-law Jonathan, as we share housing when I'm on the West Coast. Jon and I can talk about anything, and it flows through our biblical worldview. I love the way they both think, and as a couple, I find them to be unique in their age group to see all of life through the lens of Scripture. They don't fall for the fads that come and go. Their consistency is a great gift they're giving to my grandchildren.

Also, Jon has a challenging job in the building industry, working for a dear friend of mine. This son of mine (I see him as a son) latched on to our worldview and approaches his work as a son to the company. He serves in leadership to make my friend and his business successful.

They bless me greatly.

Here are some hot issues and topics on which my worldview determines my stance and leanings: euthanasia, genetic research and development advancement in medicine, stem cell research, animal rights, same-sex marriage, divorce, publicly funded education, role of the state in citizens' lives, legalization of pot, environmentalism, immigration, use of military force, national defense, gun rights, free market policies, etc...

Warning! If I got my worldview by default, thanks to my passivity, my viewpoints may be cloudy since I never considered the "Why?" question.

That list is as long as what is happening all around us. So, guys, it's time to man up and ask ourselves, "Did I get my worldview on the street because my head was in the sand, or did I intentionally build it through a rational study of the Scriptures over time?"

Here is the good news. You can tear down and rebuild your worldview with the right help and by God's grace. By the way, He really wants to give us help because He doesn't want His sons walking around like a bunch of brain-dead sheep.

Let's get to work!

The Major Elements of a Worldview

If we're serious about building a biblically based, Christ-centered worldview, these are the questions that need to be pondered and answered. First, who is God, and how did all life originate? Who is mankind and what is mankind's primary purpose on the Earth? What is truth, and what is it based upon? Then, what are the rules and ethics for society? Finally, from these, how do you develop a biblical worldview?

Start at the top.

Who is God?

Everyone has a god. Some have the right One, while many don't. The point is that we are created in the image of our Creator, so if we don't know who the One True God is, we will fabricate our own. It's in our fallen nature to be seeking for that greater being, and if we don't find it/him/her/or them, we'll make it up. Hence, you'll find humans who worship the gods of Olympus; Odin and Thor of the Norsemen, aka Vikings; Marvel and DC comic superheroes; and pop stars, even the wimpy variety. Hollywood "celebrities" are worshipped by adoring fans, and people spend $400 to own shoes branded for superstar athletes. Even the made-up vampire-zombie-mummy-Jason-demon-angel personality is held on a pedestal!

Our fascination with the undead, occult, and paranormal in film is more than fascination—it's a quest for something greater, something beyond human that fits the god-mold. It doesn't even matter if "my creation" is morally good, bad, or indifferent as long as it has powers and abilities beyond "me." This fascination is man searching for his Creator, his roots.

Why do men seek some god or a greater power in whom or what they can trust and somehow rely upon? Genesis 1:27 gives us the answer: "So God created man in His own image, in the image of God He created him; male and female He created them."

The human race is made in the image of the Great God, and after the "fall" in Genesis 3, that image was marred but not annihilated. Thus in a fallen state, we seek after our origins because it's in our spiritual DNA to do so. Without the redeeming light and life of Christ to awaken us, we will seek that source solely on a lateral, temporal, and finite level, according to the limits of our human understanding. Therefore, we will ascribe human-like attributes to our gods. The entertainment industry has capitalized upon the inherent need in every human creature with a plethora of godlike creations that do more than just entertain—they give us something to strive for, to follow.

Get the picture? There is nothing new under the sun, so humans will forever make gods in their image if they don't worship the One in whose image they are already made. Why do the *Star Wars* and *Harry Potter* films kill it at the box office? Certainly they entertain, but they also call to our inner soul, to us relating to the supernatural acts of the heroes, and we *are them* in our imaginations.

As I write this chapter, the Halloween season is underway. Today I was in a store and browsed through the costume section. I found a "satanic makeup kit" and a "zombie packet" and plenty of Jason masks. The search continues every year, every season. Then on the way home, I turned the radio on and caught the last half of the Rolling Stones' dramatic "Sympathy for the Devil." Seems I can't get away from all the man-made gods around us. And yes, I still like rock and roll.

The second commandment addresses this sinful tendency head on: "You shall not make for yourself a carved image, or any likeness of anything that is in heaven above, or that is in earth beneath, or that is in the water under the earth" (Exod. 20:4).

Even God's chosen people, when they do not put their Sovereign Lord first, will fabricate and chase after their own useless gods: "Every goldsmith is put to shame by his idols, for his images are false, and there is no breath in them. They are worthless, a work of delusion" (Jer. 10:14–15).

When Jacob was escaping Laban's tyranny, even his favorite wife Rachel, the mother of Joseph and Benjamin, fell into the trap: "Now Rachel had taken the household gods and put them in the camel's saddle" (Gen. 31:34).

Every household, then and now, has their gods. The issue being, is it the One God or the many? There is truly nothing new under the sun. It's simply easier to make a god in our image, one that we can define and control with human traits and supernatural abilities.

When Ruth told Naomi she would follow her back to Israel from Moab, Naomi had an amazing response: "See, your sister-in-law has gone back to her people and to her gods; return after your sister-in-law" (Ruth 1:15). Naomi naturally assumed Ruth would do what everyone around them did: return to the family gods. And who were these gods, and where did they originate? They were made up, like all gods, in the image of something in Creation.

God-making was an epidemic then and still is today. In fact, while Moses was receiving the tablets from the Lord, on which the Decalogue was written, the Israelites were making their own god in the form of a calf from their own gold jewelry and coin! They wanted something tangible, visible, touchable, fully understandable, without spiritual mystery or holiness, to make their worship clean, neat, and easy. After all, if we make gods in images we know and understand, there is no need to fear or awe, or even obey them, because we know they hold no power over us. This is actually a smart way to get followers. Hollywood does it all the time with superheroes, lycans, zombie slayers, etc. The action figure has powers beyond ours and can do things onscreen we can't do in real life, but they don't watch to see if we're naughty or nice. Of course, we've assigned them those powers.

Consider the Lord's warnings against the making and/or worshipping of false gods, which can take on many forms and types, whether they are inanimate, in nature, human, alien, etc.:

> Has a nation changed it gods, even though
> they are no gods? But my people have changed
> their glory for that which does not profit...

> For long ago I broke your yoke and burst
> your bonds; but you said, "I will not serve," yes,
> on every high hill and under every green tree you
> bowed down like a whore...
> (You) say to a tree, "You are my father," and
> to a stone, "You gave me birth"...
> But where are your gods that you have made
> for yourself? Let them arise if they can save you.
> (Jer. 2:11, 20, 27, 28)

The Lord is not speaking to a group of pagan druid priests. No, He is addressing the chosen people of Judah, the southern kingdom, His beloved sons and daughters.

Wow! If this tendency to invent our own gods resides in followers of Christ, what is it like across a whole society? It is out of control. People of every generation across the globe are chasing after whatever god they invent or learn from others, that calls to the lost soul within to give it something to worship and believe, even if it's hard core humanism, where man is his own god.

Can we see the huge implication here? My view and definition of God will drive everything else. Therefore, the sources I utilize to define God, Creation, and purpose are pretty important. Those sources might actually lead me to believe that God is not there, and man is purely self-determining. You'll pretty much get this on most college campuses today.

Perhaps the greatest example of this is Adam, the first man. When the serpent showed up in Genesis chapter 3, Adam used him as the source of his information and logic, upon which he made his decision: "'You will not certainly die,' the serpent said to the woman. 'For God knows that when you eat from it your eyes will be opened, and you will be like God, knowing good and evil'" (Gen. 3:4–5).

And, just like that, Adam invented the worldview of humanism, in which the human race determines and knows and becomes all it needs, because it has in it all it needs to achieve it! Of course, the serpent was speaking to Eve, while Adam was on his phone setting up his fantasy team for the game that night, but more on *this* problem later. Adam's worldview is alive and well today—in evolutionism science, celebrity gurus, self-help actualization movements, the "rights" movement of women, animals, the Earth, millenials, and on and on. They have one thing in common: man, or woman, is at the center of his, or her, own universe.

Let's follow the logical progression of Adam's autonomy, which we all inherited. First, our conclusion: all worldviews not derived from the Holy Scriptures are based upon the root of humanist philosophy—autonomy, which can be explained as follows:

> I can choose freely and wisely because I am basically a good person. Therefore, I know what is right and what is not, in my own mind.
>
> Therefore, I determine that this worldview (insert any of them here) is the right one because I chose it, and again, because I am good, wise, capable, more informed, and more advanced than the limited thinkers in the Bible.

I trust we get the drift here. We are autonomous in our fallen, depraved nature and not capable of choosing Christ and His worldview without His gracious awakening and salvation. Therefore, we choose, according to what is naturally inside our minds as the marred image in us seeks our Creator, by using an autonomous, I-know-better inclination that logically results in made-up gods. Make sense?

Simply using the serpent's rationale and information, Adam cursed the entire human race. Too bad he didn't have a biblical worldview! I somewhat jest here because if any of us were Adam, we also would have taken the bait, so let's not put all the blame on him. That said, his decision was based upon input from a certain source. Thus we ask ourselves, "What sources have I used over time to build my view of God and develop my worldview?" This will help in determining how screwed up our view is.

Honestly, a serious look at the Scriptures as they paint the picture of a purely holy, totally sovereign God who creates and rules what He makes, confronts the Adam in all of us. We don't always like what we find, because we want to choose for ourselves and be our own bosses.

Next question.

How did all life originate?

Entire ministries, and humanist-based organizations, are dedicated to answering this question. Yet each of us must confront it and resolve it, because it is a determining factor in worldview development. Are origins designed and established by a sovereign, involved God, or is it arbitrary? This ultimately determines society's view of the value of life. Is a human life more valuable than an animal's life? If not, welcome to the animal rights movement. Does human life begin at conception?

Today people make a fortune providing special burial or preserving services for the deceased and well-loved animals with owners who have elevated them to the same life-value level as humans. Perhaps, they have instead lowered our human value. This is *not meant* to bash extreme animal lovers—I'm just pointing out how worldview questions drive our values, behavior, and spending habits. I know veterinarians who make some serious money on ACL surgery for someone's special dog. Hey, I'm all for capitalism, so if they can capitalize on a growing worldview movement, so be it. Maybe I should have gone to vet school.

The individual beliefs of the origins of life for humans and the animal world will drive the image in which humans view themselves, the value of their lives, and ultimately, their purpose on this Earth. If an Almighty Creator God did not create us, then none of this is clear.

Who is mankind?

If we were created in the image of a Creator, then our nature is found somewhere in that Creator's plan and work. Then comes perhaps the biggest question we face: "Is man basically good?" Think about it. If I follow Christ as a Christian and somehow believe in the inherent goodness of human beings, then I am capable of sound self-determination and decision-making with little outside help. I really don't need all that accountability to elders that Paul and Peter wrote about, and I can choose what church to join or not join based solely upon my own observations. Obviously it goes far beyond this, but the implications are enormous. Today's violent and vile crime is off the charts, and no one has answers for the causes, and therefore, the solutions.

On the other hand, if I believe all humans are totally depraved and incapable of moral change of themselves or society, my approach to society's problems is quite different. Then, I recognize cause and effect in a family, neighborhood, and society. If man is inherently good, as today's culture teaches, then understanding the roots of behavioral problems becomes a can of worms, and we become increasingly dependent upon "experts" who we hope will give us answers but who continually struggle to explain good, bad, and evil. This question, who is mankind, is a major component of a worldview.

What is mankind's primary purpose on Earth?

Here is the "why" question again: Why are we here? How I answer questions A, B, and C leads me to D. If the Bible is my source, then it is responsible to answer and explain how men are to live with purpose. Many folks get their view on this why question through mixed sources like a Bible, a psychology teacher, a favorite talk show host, the best-sellers book lists, action movies, etc. It just happens without us realizing it, like the frog in a pot of cold water that slowly boils to death when the pot is put over a flame. He never sees it coming. What a sucker! Wait a minute, that could be me!

What is truth, and what is it based upon?

Today's culture is in a virtual civil war over this question: what is truth? Here is the problem for a man. If he marries and has children, who teaches his children what Pontius Pilate wanted to know...what is truth? Is it the health teacher at school, the youth leader, the guidance counselor? Listen, friends, if dad waits that long for his young ones to be taught the truth, they already have their views on it pretty established. Why do you think *Sesame Street* was so popular and so are endless children's stories and games? Because they aren't just virtual babysitters—they're truth-tellers (from their perspective, of course). Public broadcasting is actually a genius idea, because the programmers can produce pure humanism in cute cartoon form, and no one can stop them—it's free state-run mentoring in the form of entertainment without the hassle of accountability to private sponsorship.

Anyway, truth today is virtually based upon opinion, which is derived from both experience and the influence of louder sources. I've lost count of the Christians that have said, "I feel this is what the Lord is trying to tell us in these Scripture verses," to which I want to respond, "Who cares how you *feel* about it? Is that what the text actually says?" Here's another thought often vocalized: "I just can't believe a loving God would allow something like that to happen"; not, "Based upon what I have studied in the Scriptures in [insert verse], I have discovered that man actually has a greater responsibility for his actions, and their impact on the generations that follow, than I initially thought."

The former example above is emotional thinking, while the latter is an objective thought process. One is based upon opinion and stimuli, while the other finds it basis solely in the Scriptures. Which will it be for you?

What are the rules and ethics for society?

Do we really need to go here? How many of us know the difference between ethics and *my morals*, or how they are determined and then applied to a people. Or, if the current condition of society's ethics is off, then how does God fix it, and what is our role? By the way, society's ethics *are* off, in case you've been in a coma. See what I mean—who wants to tackle this one? Yet, what "I believe" drives how I live in a culture without ethical standards and makes me an influencer, not an influencee.

People who understand ethics have an advantage because they are better suited at social problem-solving, in that they adhere to a consistent and objective standard that is applicable in all situations life throws at us.

What are the jurisdictional patterns that work for a society or nation?

We shall see in our journey that God has established a logical and predictable order to the way society is structured and governed. Again, today's anarchist and humanist have left objective thinking in the rearview mirror, and the result is confusing and inconsistent opinions as to what does and doesn't work in a society, a family, a business, a church, or any institution. Jurisdictional thinking gives those who possess it an edge in how and why things work or break down. Stay tuned.

How to Develop a Biblical Worldview

Basically addressing the following major issues will do the trick.

A. Determine the nature of God's kingdom:
    Is Christ's kingdom rule present, future, or both?
    How far does Christ's kingdom extend today on Earth?
    Is it everywhere, or within the church?
    Did Adam lose the Earth, and does the devil rule until Jesus returns?
B. If His reign is present and total everywhere, then Christians must filter every issue of life through the Holy Scriptures, and this includes all private, public, socioeconomic, governmental, physical, and emotional issues, etc.
C. If His reign is present and total and everywhere, then the Christian's active involvement in society, at all levels and in all ways, is a normal part of life.
D. If the Scriptures teach a dualism—the complete separation of the physical and the material—then involvement in society is optional.

The big issue here is "calling." Is "calling" a spiritual ministry within the redeemed community, or does it include vocational destiny in the marketplace, public arena, medicine, law, etc.? In other words, is going to work Monday morning a holy calling from God?

Now What?

In that this book is not purely a study on worldview but rather a search in Scripture for who the man is created to be and what he looks like being it, the chapters following will unpack this in the context of the parameters and questions posed above. Our worldview will develop as we march on.

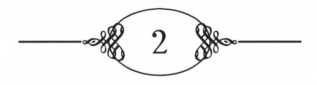

Covenant—The Worldview by Which We Should Live

When I was the pastor at Covenant Life Church in the nineties, I started a meeting for men and their sons at 5:30 a.m. on Saturdays. What was I thinking? To make matters worse, we lived in Upstate New York. Do you have any idea how cold it is at 5:00 a.m. on a Saturday in January? My boys were thrilled to get dragged out of their warm beds.

An amazing thing happened though—most of the men in the church began to show up and brought their sons with them. We made it inconvenient because we wanted guys that wanted to be there. This was not a men's breakfast club. We established commitment terms concerning attendance and participation, and we tackled challenging doctrinal and social issues that confront men. We also intentionally involved the young men and held ceremonies to welcome new brothers to the gathering. Together we learned to think objectively about Scripture as we challenged one another, and we grew into a brotherhood—men in covenant with one another, bound together through our covenant with the Lord Jesus Christ, who called us to be as one.

It went off the rails when it became too exclusive in our minds. It was so unique and special to us that we guarded it more than we shared it (my bad). The point? The unique and special qualities were there because it was based upon us being in a covenant around our purpose together. I don't think any of us ever experienced such a thing before. We studied, worked, prayed, built, and grew with each other and our sons, who we treated as young men, and not as teenage adolescent brats. We learned that being in covenant is inconvenient but life-altering in its multigenerational, sacrificial, and mutual properties. This was not a group—it was a band of brothers. I still miss it.

This story begs the question: "What is covenant?" The word *covenant* is too overused today, often without biblical context, but the motives are usually sincere. Twenty-five Christian men may give twenty-five different answers to our question. The only answer that matters is what the Scriptures say about it, so let's take a look.

Jesus said, "I am the way, the truth, and the life. No one comes to the Father except by Me" (John 14:6). What is Jesus's only way for us to relate to our Creator? That's right—through covenant. I trust we realize both the entire Old and New Testaments are "covenants"—literally, it's what they are called. If the entire testament is a covenant, there must be something pretty serious to the concept.

So here is our basis: covenant is the only way God relates to us humans, and these covenants are the established pattern by which our lives are to be lived. Hence, covenant is at the core of a biblical worldview. It is a solemn compact that binds two parties together in holy fear, awe, and ongoing renewal, according to its terms.

After the fall, God initiated a series of covenants, with Noah (Gen. 6:17), Abraham (Gen. 15–17), Moses and Israel (Exod. 19–24), and David (2 Sam. 7:8–16). These covenants do not stand alone but are links in the chain of the covenant of grace, which culminates at Calvary at the atoning death of the Lord Jesus Christ.

Consider God calling Abram to leave his homeland and follow the Lord, by becoming the progenitor of His people, and the only way God would relate with, and to, His people was through covenant:

> Now the Lord said to Abram, "Go from your country and your kindred and your father's house to the land I will show you. And I will make of you a great nation, and I will bless you and make your name great, so that you will be

29

a blessing. I will bless those who bless you, and him who dishonors you I will curse, and in you all the families of the Earth shall be blessed." (Gen. 12:1–3)

I will make you exceedingly fruitful, and I will make nations of you, and kings will come forth from you. I will establish My *covenant* between Me and you and your descendants after you throughout their generations for an ever-lasting *covenant*, to be God to you and to your descendants after you. I will give to you and to your descendants after you, the land of your sojournings, all the land of Canaan, for an ever-lasting possession; and I will be their God.

God said further to Abraham, "Now as for you, you shall keep My *covenant*, you and your descendants after you throughout their genera-tions. This is My *covenant*, which you shall keep, between Me and you and your descendants after you: every male among you shall be circumcised. (Gen. 17:6–10; emphasis added).

Notice God didn't tell Abram He had a plan, and Abram needed to follow Him. Rather He established a holy compact between Himself and a portion of the human race that would never end. Wow, that is fairly serious. Even more amazing is the nature of the oath the Lord made in this covenant:

After this, the word of the Lord came to Abram in a vision: "Do not be afraid, Abram. I am your shield, your very great reward."

But Abram said, 'Sovereign Lord, what can you give me since I remain childless and the one who will inherit my estate is Eliezer of Damascus?' And Abram said, "You have given me no children; so a servant in my household will be my heir."

Then the word of the Lord came to him: "This man will not be your heir, but a son who is your own flesh and blood will be your heir." He took him outside and said, "Look up at the sky and count the stars—if indeed you can count them." Then He said to him, "So shall your offspring be. Abram believed the Lord, and he credited it to him as righteousness." (Gen. 15:1–6)

Whoa, hold on here! Abram never even offered a sacrifice, he just believed, and he is counted as righteous? That sounds like new covenant (aka New Testament) promise to me. How many times did Jesus, and then Paul, tell us our salvation and righteousness depended upon nothing we could offer but rather the finished work of Christ? Our job is to believe, to have faith, and nothing else. This is the fruit of the new covenant. This is also the pathway for Abram and his descendants: faith.

The text further explains how this can be so in the covenant God is making with Abram:

> So the Lord said to him (Abram), "Bring me a heifer, a goat and a ram, each three years old, along with a dove and a young pigeon." Abram brought all these to him, cut them in two and arranged the halves opposite each other; the birds, however he did not cut in half. The birds of prey came down on the carcasses, but Abram drove them away.
>
> As the sun was setting, Abram fell into a deep sleep, and a thick dreadful darkness came over him...
>
> When the sun had set and darkness had fallen, a smoking firepot with a blazing torch appeared and passed between the pieces. On that day the

> Lord made a covenant with Abram and said, 'To your descendants I give this land, from the Wadi to Egypt to the great river, the Euphrates—the land of the Kenites...(Gen. 15:9–19)

Friend, what did Abram do while the covenant ceremony was being played out and sealed? He did what we all do and added what we all add—nothing. In fact, he slept. He rested while God did the work. And the result was that God promised Abram and his descendants everything He offered him when He called him in Genesis 12. Yet this was more than a promise. The Lord God passed between the slain animals that were cut in half. Through this act, He essentially declared, "May I end up like these dead animals if this covenant is not fulfilled."

Are you kidding me? God is guaranteeing the covenant with His own life, which of course became a reality when Jesus offered Himself on the cross. Can we see the incredible connection from Genesis to Christ, the links of a chain, the covenant of grace? The entire Old Testament is a chronicle: the playing out of these covenant links with the patriarchs. They are not stand-alone stories; rather, they are the story of the great covenant by which the Creator God relates to His people, which thankfully today is through the finished work of Jesus Christ.

Therefore, today God calls us to covenant with Him just as He did the chosen people of the Old Testament. The difference? The final sacrifice has been made, and His name is Jesus. Therefore, all that we do is in His name, because we are bound in covenant to Him and the Father through His blood. Get it? We are still in covenant, with God and one another, just like our spiritual ancestors, and we always will be until the end of days. Incredible.

As the way of the Lord is covenant, the Scriptures set the stage for how life will be lived going forward, for all the institutions or spheres in society, via the principles of covenant:

- The Individual
- The Family
- The Church

- The Marketplace
- The Civil Government (we call it "the government" today, but more on this later)

Because it is so critical that the covenant way be followed, God basically said, "May I be as these dead animals through which I am passing if this covenant is broken." He put the onus on Himself, not Abraham! Let's see why.

The Nature of Covenant

Pastor Tim Keller, who did a masterful job in explaining the unique nature of covenant, once taught that "covenant is infinitely more intimate and personal than any legal relationship you have ever seen, and it is infinitely more binding, enduring and accountable than any personal relationship."

Pastor Keller shows us that covenant is a genius blend of law and love that sadly is lost in our culture:

It is more intimate and personal because it is more binding.
And…
It is more binding because it's intimately personal.

Notice the "Both/And" nature of covenant. Law, meet love; and love, meet law. It's called covenant, and there is nothing like it in any other worldview, philosophy, or social construct. This is actually freeing because its binding nature creates a safe place for the parties to be themselves with secure knowledge of what's ahead in the journey.

Essentially then, a covenant is a relationship between two or more parties based upon a compact that binds the parties together through a sacred oath. Notice both the relational and legal sides of any biblical covenant.

The Uniqueness of Covenant

Firstly, covenant is guaranteed by the Covenant-Maker. The original covenant between God and Adam is referred to by theologians as the "covenant of works," in which Adam had to obey the terms for the covenant to remain intact in its agreed upon form. After the fall, God instituted the covenant of grace, as cited above. The difference is that the Lord God swore by His own life that this covenant would not be annulled—remember His oath in passing between the row of animals split in two? Thus, grace is guaranteed to the human parties in these covenants. They are links in the chain of the covenant of grace.

He gave signs of His promise guarantee: the rainbow, circumcision, the Decalogue, the temple, the cross, and bread and wine. These were different administrations of the covenant of grace, which culminated in the atoning sacrifice of the Lord Jesus Christ, sealing all who believe in His merciful redemption.

This doesn't mean that those before us and we ourselves have not violated the covenant, because we all have, being sinners saved by His grace. It does mean biblical covenant carries the uniqueness of renewal when sanctions are applied due to human disobedience. This means that no matter my sin, renewal is given through a contrite prayer or act of repentance, but this *doesn't* mean there are no consequences to my stupid behavior. Rather, in the midst of a harvest, I can find renewal in my relationship with my Creator and be in oneness with Him and fellow believers. There is no agreement or contract on Earth that carries such an incredible redemptive property in it as biblical covenant does.

Secondly, covenant is generational. The other major unique property to a biblical covenant is that it is generational by its very nature. In fact, God shows Himself to be the ultimate "Family Man," as He sent His own Son, not a commando, an angel, nor a secret agent. He sent family. Let us consider God's perspective through His language:

> "For God so loved the world that He sent His only begotten Son" (John 3:16).

> "And God blessed them. And God said to them, 'Be fruitful and multiply and fill the Earth and subdue it" (Gen. 1:28).

"This is the book of the generations of Adam…" (Gen. 5).

"And God said to Noah and his sons with him, 'Behold, I establish my covenant with you and your offspring after you'" (Gen. 9:8–9).

"Then the Lord appeared to Abram and said, 'To your offspring I will give this land'" (Gen. 12:7).

"And I will establish my covenant between me and you and your offspring after you for an everlasting covenant" (Gen. 17:7).

"Then Isaac called Jacob and blessed him… 'May He [God] give the blessing of Abraham to you and your offspring with you" (Gen. 28:1, 4).

"And God said [to Moses], 'I am the God of your father, the God of Abraham, the God of Isaac, and the God of Jacob'" (Exod. 3:6).

Note: Jacob had been dead for about four hundred years by now!

"Say this to the people of Israel, 'The Lord, the God of your fathers, the God of Abraham, the God of Isaac, and the God of Jacob, has sent me to you.' This is my name forever, and thus I am to be remembered throughout all generations" (Exod. 3:15).

"The Lord was with Jehoshaphat, because he walked in the earlier ways of his father David" (2 Chron. 17:3).

Friends, we need to understand that David died about one hundred years before Jehoshaphat became king, but the Lord referred to him as the latter's "father." Jesus is the God of history, and when He looks at one generation, He sees many before and after, in the sense that each life is a seed for those who will follow, and the terms of the covenant dramatically impact subsequent generations, not even born yet.

Can we see the dilemma in our culture in light of this truth? Today, hardly anyone thinks multigenerationally, and thus no one lives that way. Yet, if it's the Lord's way, why don't we? Can we see how covenant is at the core of a biblical worldview?

I love this next example, as it shows the power of the blessing of covenant that lasts for generations, in spite of our wickedness. Referring to Abijam, king over Judah several generations after David's death, we read, "And he walked in all the sins that his father did before him, and his heart was not wholly true to the Lord his God, as the heart of David his father. Nevertheless, for David's sake the Lord his God gave him a lamp in Jerusalem" (1 Kings 15:3–4).

We need to stop right now, hit the floor, and thank the Lord for the "nevertheless" mercies shown to us because of the covenant He has made!

Now we need a little New Testament confirmation. Jesus is dealing with the Sadducees who claimed there is no resurrection, and the Lord says, "And as for the resurrection of the dead, have you not read what was said to you by God: 'I am the God of Abraham, and the God of Isaac, and the God of Jacob'? He is not the God of the dead, but of the living" (Matt. 22:31–32).

He could have just referred to the "God of Abraham," since Abraham was the original patriarch, but Jesus echoes what the Lord shows us in the Old Testament language:

"As He passed by, He saw a man blind from birth. And His disciples asked him, 'Rabbi, who sinned, this man or his parent, that he was born blind?' Jesus answered, 'It was not that this man sinned, or his parents, but that the works of God might be displayed in him" (John 9:1–3).

Jesus is not dismissing the effects of original sin nor the sins of the fathers upon ensuing generations, as Scripture taught, but rather explains to the twelve that in this case, it is a different cause.

And now, my favorite, concerning Levi, the great-grandson of Abraham, and what he "got" when Abraham tithed to Melchizedek: "One might even say that Levi himself, who receives tithes, paid tithes through Abraham, for he was still in the loins of his ancestor when Melchizedek met him" (Heb. 7:9–10).

Dare we ask ourselves, when we refuse to give our tithes and offerings to the Lord, "For which of my descendants am I causing major problems before he or she is even conceived?" Or, if you are generous, do you thank the Lord for His covenantal blessings on your great-grandchildren as you walk in faithfulness as His son?

Notice below both the continuity and generational properties of covenant: "The unbelieving husband is made holy because of his wife, and the unbelieving wife is made holy because of her husband. Otherwise your children would be unclean, but as it is, they are holy" (1 Cor. 7:14).

Now, *holy* means "set apart" for God and not under condemnation, while *unclean* is not a moral impurity but rather separated from the community—outside and under judgment. Therefore, simply because one spouse believes, the benefits of the covenant extend to the other spouse in the marriage covenant and to the generations. The children are secured from judgment because the faith of the parent marks them. We see this pattern in Genesis when God established his generational covenant with Abram and told him to circumcise every male as a sign that they are secure in the elect community of faith. Neither the children in Genesis, nor in Corinth, had the adult ability to reason and believe, but saving promises were extended to them because of the parents. In fact, without dad and mom, the children were helpless and hopeless. *This is generational thinking!* Do we as parents take our faith this seriously and see it as a covenantal blessing of promise to our children?

There is more where this came from, but we get a clear picture and message that the Lord designed the family, and thus He designed a generational strategy, to be the engine that drives a society, for good and for bad. And who is responsible for leading the family, as described in the Scriptures? That's right, men—us.

God's plan begins with the man, who is the "gatekeeper" of his family, who sets the stage for all who follow. Without a context, one could get spooked by this statement, but it is simply the Lord's design. This, however, does not discount the amazing single mothers who give their lives for their children, whom God includes in this plan.

The Elements of Covenant

Reverend Ray Sutton wrote a comprehensive analysis of what makes up a biblical covenant in his book *That You May Prosper*. I recommend it to all men. We have just seen how covenant is both legally and relationally binding. Sutton captures this in his book, showing that there are five main points/parts to a covenant:

1. Transcendence—who is the initiator, and who is in charge?
2. Hierarchy—who carries delegated authority from God and to whom do I report?
3. Ethics—what are the terms and rules of the covenant?
4. Sanctions—what happens if I obey or disobey the rules?
5. Succession—how is it renewed and then passed on generationally?

The brilliance of this straightforward pattern is that it applies to all spheres and/or institutions in a society, whether men are aware of it or not.

- Family
- Church
- Business (all private sector activities)
- State (the public sector—the civil arena, typically called "the government" today)
- Volunteer, charitable, nonprofit groups

Any group, organization (large, medium, or small), company, town hall, sheriff's department, law office, hospital, university, performing arts conglomerate, day care, school, little league, small business, home, you name it, operates under the five simple points of covenant.

In other words, this is the pattern the Lord established, the principles of which are always at work in any organization at any time, regardless of whether that organization is dedicated to Christ's cause. It's simply the boilerplate He made, and as we consider the five points, it's simple to see that they are applied on a regular basis in a hospital, auto repair shop, nightclub, gang, team, church, and courtroom. Someone leads, someone represents the leader, rules are established, consequences and benefits follow, and it either has a future or it dissolves. This fifth point plays out when leaders ignore the future—this gives the disenfranchised followers "opportunity" to look elsewhere.

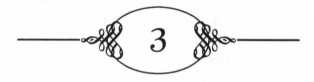

A Man, His Family, and the Covenant Model

A covenantal worldview is a great gift from the Lord to a man, as it shows him his role and gives him a clear pattern as to how to lead his family. Let's therefore take a look at a picture of the family through this pattern of a five-point covenant model. This will give us a type of aerial view of the man as the gatekeeper which is a term you'll being hear more about as we push through. We are the gatekeepers, as designed by our Creator God, and His favor and grace is upon us to be it and do it. This is not a demand for men's rights or demeaning women in any way. It's simply an honest look at the Scriptural design for the man.

Here we go. We'll look at each of the five points in an applicable way for the man.

Transcendence (or Sovereignty)

The Lord God is sovereign over all creation, as its Creator and Covenant Keeper. While He transcends all things made, as He is not part of His creation, He is at the same time involved with His people to guide and govern according to His plan.

Thus, God is the creator of the family as the core institution in society that feeds all other spheres. When the family breaks down (and it has), then all other organizations suffer with weak and confused men and women that cannot do good work, handle pressure, resolve conflict, and lead. I often use the labor union movement as an example. The unions served an important purpose in the early to mid-twentieth century in confronting oppression, mismanagement, and greed on the part of owners. The movement won certain rights and a general improvement in working conditions and wages. A problem arose when union leaders realized they were driving the agenda and the same power lust in the owners infected them. As a result, demands got out of control but owners had little recourse, and union power grew. As it grew, so did the depraved corruption of attitude in both union leaders and workers. In all my years, I never heard a guy in a union speak glowingly of the "bosses." Rather, this is what I heard:

"Those effing bosses wouldn't be anywhere without us."

"The foreman is a moron, who's always got his head up his _____."

"My boss doesn't know the first thing about what we do. He's screwed without us."

Now some of this might have been true, but the issue was the attitude—that the worker was doing management a huge favor by gracing them with his presence, especially when he worked over forty hours for double wages.

A funny thing then happened. Japan started selling high-quality automobiles and trucks in the US thanks to bad tariff laws. People started buying foreign-made cars and Detroit's economy got squeezed. The only problem was that union workers didn't care because they had guarantees via the collective bargaining agreement. "So what if the ship is taking water? I get my overtime and eight weeks' vacation and full medical and dental!" The union man had become a hireling, working to get all he could rather than to make the company successful. After a few beers, some of the guys I knew actually seemed to want management to fail, obviously not connecting the dots, thanks to cheap beer. The richer the unions got, the lower the quality of the product, because wages and benefits were guaranteed.

This is where the gatekeeper comes in. Dad's job is to instill in his sons and daughters a sense of sonship in their vocational callings, in which they are placed by God to make that business better every day. Instead, the kids grew into takers, dad bought the six-packs, and they'd commiserate over the loser bosses they were all stuck with. Weak men produce bad workers. The Lord designed it to be better.

Hierarchy (or Representation)

This is probably the most important principle among the five points. Hierarchy means that the Lord delegates His authority to authorized representatives, so that to exercise proper authority, one must be under authority. Every institution has a hierarchy of representatives, and in the family, the man is the "gatekeeper": the one entrusted with governing authority over the family as keeper, protector, provider, and shepherd. This empowers the wife's authority through proper representation; it does not nullify her authority in any way.

As a man walks under delegated authority, he can safely lead his own family. He doesn't just exercise authority, but the covenant makes him responsible to be accountable to his wife and children in the way he loves, leads, and prepares. In other words, if hubby is blowing it, he answers to his delegated authority to make things right—his wife has a safe place of appeal if her man has gone off the rails.

Let me explain using my own journey. When Sandra and I married, I was more than rough around the edges, having been saved by God's mercies out of a rebellious and rough lifestyle. I met her soon after my conversion, and the Lord blessed the relationship so that we were married five months later—not much time to work on my sanctification! We realize now that if she knew some of the baggage I carried, she probably would have married a nice musician, so God hid it from her and she said yes. Suffice to say that I was not always a kind and loving husband and often spoke in a hurtful and disrespectful tone to her. She'd be hurt and I couldn't understand why, because that type of speech was "normal" to me at that time.

By God's grace, I was submitted to the pastor of the church, and Sandra blew the whistle on me. I told him and his wife and our Bible teacher, who became a spiritual father to me, that I'd do whatever necessary to change. They came up with a plan—they'd keep an eye on me, and when I crossed the disrespect line, they would call me on it. I agreed; after all, how tough could it be? You don't want to know.

One time I got pulled aside on a Sunday morning just before the service began by the Bible teacher's wise and kind wife, and she let me have it about the way I spoke to Sandra as we entered the building. Ouch. I could go on, but the key was my accountability to them, which in turn provided Sandra both a safe place and a tangible hope that I would change. Four decades later, I think I have changed (ask her).

This is the piece of representation that provides for course corrections and ensures a safe environment for all family members. Listen, men think they are better, cooler, wiser, or more "okay" than they really are. Remember, guys, self-deception is every man's gift. So the pathway for appeal is a crucial element in any covenant and perhaps especially so for a wife and the children when dad gets caught up in his false "self" and just assumes he's fine. Sadly, our insecurities breed this uptight self-view, because we really don't want to be found out.

However, in a true covenant relationship with real representation, the place of appeal tells a wife that her man means business about truly being the husband and father the Lord meant him to be. A wife is secure in her place and will stand with her husband in all of his ideas, including the misadventures. I speak from experience, as Sandra has called my pastor a number of times over the years—with my permission to do so *without* having to check with me first—and when he checks in with me, I'm ready to listen and man up to whatever problem I caused. That's because the Lord's blessing and favor is upon such a relationship, and His grace is very present for the man to change and grow.

What was all that? Simply representation at work—my delegated authority, my wife, acted in love within the covenant to keep me accountable, so that I could and would eventually exercise my delegated authority in the home properly. Even today, after all these years, Sandra knows she can pick up the phone and rat me out to my pastor if I'm way out of line. My adult children also know this, and they have confronted me at times when I abused my role, because they knew that in the family covenant I was accountable to them to listen. This is why representation in the covenant works, for as my wise pastor once said, "We each have enough self-deception in us to last us a lifetime." How true, my friend, how true. Honest representative authority gives me eyes where I am blind.

Once the man is accountable, the family can function smoothly under godly government. When a man seeks proper use of delegated authority, his wife and children are authorized and empowered to function in their strengths as they also represent Christ and one another.

Remember, when an authority figure is under real authority, who is also under authority, appeal is a safe pathway to renewal and maturity. A wife and the sons and daughters can trust their hearts to their husband and dad, as he has shown himself accountable and vulnerable.

Now, isn't this a major crisis in our culture today? Clueless, insecure men turn to no one but themselves, because of their insecurity, and they resort to control through anger, neglect, or abuse, to get a son or daughter to "get in line." Jesus gave us something so much better, so much clearer, and so much simpler to apply.

Ethics (or Rules)

According to Dictionary.com, ethics is "a complex of moral precepts held or rules of conduct followed by an individual." This is what got Peter Pan and the Lost Boys all tight in their boxers, because they didn't want responsibility: "I won't grow up. No, I never ever will." Today's anarchist sheep on the college campus, in a trendy coffee "experience," or the twenty-something default Marxist, drinking the nonsense on social media, all have the same problem as Pete and the boys. I've heard countless people talk about churches being trapped in "dead religion" because they have rules. Are you kidding me?

The culture is saturated in a worldview of humanist relativism in which there exist no absolute truths, which, of course, plays into every man and woman's autonomous anarchy. Without Christ people want to be boss, and relativism allows them to make up their own rules (or lack thereof), without consequences. Of course confusion now reigns in the legal and political arenas because objective standards can no longer be established without someone being branded as divisive, racist, or guilty of hate crimes. When our worldview does not submit totally to Jesus and His Holy Scripture, relativism and disaster reign.

We need look no further than Adam, who had a clear job description to work and protect the garden, and one rule: don't eat from one tree. How did his anarchy work out? It never does, because the right rules actually form a foundation for a safe environment.

Likewise, a man who holds clear ethics regarding his family doesn't have to guess about what to do or how to do it when action is needed in the marriage, the children, finances, health, you name it. Remember this: healthy government precedes peace, and good governing requires a base of ethics to guide those who govern.

"There shall be no end to the increase of His government and of peace, [He shall rule] on the throne of David and over his kingdom, to establish it and to uphold it with justice and righteousness from that time forward and forevermore. The zeal of the Lord of hosts will accomplish this" (Isa. 9:7).

Notice how Isaiah links peace with Jesus ruling His kingdom, upholding it with justice and righteousness forever. Men are called to govern in the home, using God's rules, which are found in the Holy Scriptures—this is not real complicated, friends.

Let's get familiar with the proper definition of the word *government*, so when we see it in ensuing chapters, we'll understand it in proper context. *Noah Webster's 1828 Dictionary* defines government as "exercise of authority; direction, restraint, rule..."—(a) "over actions of men in communities according to constitutions," and (b) "by a parent or householder."

Notice it is not "the government" (i.e., the federal or state or local authorities, etc.) nor is it politics. Thus, a husband and father must govern, or someone or something else will!

Let's observe government in action in the Scriptures, as Paul is directing Timothy how to bring government, by using proper rule and restraint, to potentially dangerous men and their false teachings. Paul says, "As I urged you when I was going to Macedonia, remain at Ephesus that you may charge certain persons not to teach any different doctrine, nor to devote themselves to myths and endless genealogies" (1 Tim. 1:3–4).

Firstly, notice that Paul is authorizing Timothy to represent him as the overseer at the church of Ephesus. This is the second point of the covenant at work: representation. Secondly, he directs him to do two things that require the exercise of authority. He is to command (charge) these people to stop their teachings. And he is to direct them away from certain viewpoints and toward what Paul has taught about Christ. This is clear use of authority, without apology, but from a redemptive motive, that which is to help these deceived men and to protect the congregation.

We will address God's governments further in a while, but now consider an example many of us have experienced. Have you been in a grocery or department store and experienced the tyrannical child, around ages two to four, ruling over mom or dad, to the point where dagger eyes and whispering threats leak from the clueless parents. This is simply an example of children having no healthy government in their lives, so they lack self-restraint and cannot help but disobey. In fact, the more a parent threatens children with some form of discipline such as no video, no cell phone, or no favorite program—you know, the real harsh stuff—and never follow through, the more they teach their children to ignore governing authority and act out their own anarchistic tendencies.

Consider this example: I am on a plane in an aisle seat, and two rows ahead of me, diagonally across is a young boy—I estimate between two and three years of age—in the aisle seat. Next to him is his dad. Before takeoff the little scoundrel launched into an Olympic-sized fit. I gave him a 9.5—a real winning performance. This fit went unchecked by his dad. Once the smoke cleared and most of us passengers around them had become desperate for some quiet, his dad tried to bribe him with various sugar-high-inducing foods. Eventually the boy ran out of gas and quieted down. Can you guess what the father did during his son's emotional convulsions? If you thought he put on his headphones and ignored the little rebel… then, bingo! You guessed it!

Now if godly government, meaning healthy leadership with restraint, brings peace, then the lack of it breeds chaos, especially in the souls of little children, whose conscience and self-control mechanisms are in the embryo stages of development. It was obvious the dad had no idea what good government should look like. Had he been practicing and applying government to his son's soul at home over the previous months, the boy's soul would be at peace, his conscience clear, and his obedience-meter firing on all cylinders.

God made the gatekeeper to cause this to happen with his children. Today, the little ruffians run the show. When these unrestrained young humanists grow up with no idea how to rule their own souls and resolve their own consciences from guilt, what do you think will happen? Well, some become philosophy professors and others become psychologists to try to figure out why everybody is so messed up today in our culture. This is why mental health medicine sales have gone through the roof. That said, I appreciate that some folks really care enough to train their kids so they might help people in need. Others, however, will learn their lifestyle and crafts on the streets, in bars, in the office, or in the shop. Some will become killers, rapists, thieves, or sociopaths, while others will run for office and get elected.

The false teachers at Ephesus needed government, just like these children. It may not have been a pleasant task to Timothy, but if he didn't love these men enough to apply government, they were heading over the proverbial cliff in their self-deception. Our children will find that path if we don't govern. I'm not saying it's always a fun ride, but it is a life-changing and life-protecting one.

Sanctions (Rewards and Punishments)

Sanctions are another real crowd-pleaser in our humanist driven culture, because if society no longer ascribes to absolute ethics, then how can anyone be sure what restraint, or punishment should be applied when rules are broken—especially if "his rules aren't my rules"? It's gone so far that legal action has been taken to determine which type of capital punishment is cruel, and which is not, which of course makes no sense. You see, we have no idea where to draw lines nor how to apply sanctions that can provide redemption which would come from some pain or discipline that actually brings restorative benefits to an offender, even a child. Once upon a time, we used the Ten Commandments.

As we look further at Paul's instruction to his son Timothy, Paul shows us the application of serious sanctions, and his reason behind it, after encouraging Timothy to keep steady his faith and maintain a good conscience: "By rejecting this [faith and conscience], some have made shipwreck of their faith, among whom are Hymenaeus and Alexander, whom I have handed over to Satan that they may learn not to blaspheme" (1 Tim. 1:19–20).

This is serious governmental action. Paul pronounces judgment upon two men promoting blasphemy, and he excommunicates them, turning them over to Satan. His motive is "that they may learn not to blaspheme."

Let me make a few observations here. First, representative authority must be carried and understood. Paul can't just hand somebody over to the devil without the authority to do so. He carried representative authority, point two in the covenant. Paul is not sending idle threats; this is sober and proper punishment for breaking the rules. For example, Paul commanded the Corinthian church to excommunicate a man sleeping with his stepmother (1 Cor. 5:1–5). Discipline is a normal part of community life, be it the family, church, team, or business. If rules are not enforced, rebellion and chaos are the fruit. Remember the parents in the grocery store?

Second, the motive is godly and kind, redemptive in nature, and not cruel—for deliverance from the bondage in which they are caught. This redemption should be the motive of every dad with his children. The examples I've provided were only looking at the negative sanctions (punishments) for the sake of making a point. On the flipside, blessings and rewards come to those who follow the family way, and as a reminder, this "way" should be based upon the teachings of the Holy Scriptures, not just dad's opinions.

Third, consider the nature of responsibility. Jesus often taught through parables, and in His parable of the talents (Matt. 25:14–30), He proclaims this lesson: "His master said to him, 'Well done, good and faithful servant. You have been faithful over a little; I will set you over much. Enter into the joy of your master'" (v 23). Is this not what we long for our children to embrace? In training my sons and daughters, I called this the "*law of progressive responsibility*" and endeavored to reward them with greater opportunity when they demonstrated more responsibility. This is the fourth point of the covenant at work in the positive.

Recently, our youngest, Jake, finished high school. He just happens to be a darn good baseball player, and I told him a few years back that all of life is connected—if he showed himself responsible in academics, work around the house, and respect toward others, I would have his back as he played ball. Jake "got it" along the way and now works his tail off on the field, in the gym, and even with the books (he still doesn't like math). Thus, his mom and I are happy to invest in his dream.

Remember, however, that there are two sides to every coin—if all sanctions are rewards and no discipline is ever applied, we will raise self-centered, spoiled brats. Jake has been far from perfect, and we've had to bring the hammer down at times. How he responded determined what would happen next.

Listen, friend, if Paul saw turning people over to Satan to destroy the sin in them as proper governmental sanctions, should not we dads take this pretty seriously?

Succession (Renewal—Passing It On)

When I turned sixteen, I got a job pumping gas at a local repair shop. This was long before self-service—you got your gas and your repairs at the same garage. Across the street was a collision shop, and the owner had a 1965 Mustang convertible with a 289-cubic-inch engine, white leather seats, and a white top. Yes, sir!

The only problem was the engine was great but the body was rusted, the seats torn, and the top in bad shape. In Upstate New

York, the towns salt the roads in the winter, and salt rusts metal. He also had a hardtop Mustang, same year, with a blown engine but good exterior. So I bought both of them and spent the summer stripping both cars and putting the good parts from the hardtop on the convertible. I fixed the seats, had the top repaired, did all the priming and sanding prep work, and then had it painted. When I picked it up, it looked like a new car! Why? It went through a renewal process, and it was a painful one for a sixteen-year-old guy with no money to spare, but it was "like new"!

Is this not at the core of what the Lord Jesus does for us? We "were dead in the trespasses and sins in which (we) once walked...and were by nature children of wrath, like the rest of mankind. But God, being rich in mercy, because of the great love with which he loved us, even when we were dead in our trespasses, made us alive together with Christ—by grace you have been saved" (Eph. 2:1, 3–5).

I have probably read this a thousand times in thirty-nine years of walking with Christ, and it still blows my mind. From death comes life. The old and useless are made new and full of purpose. This is you and I. This should be how we approach our families—with a generational perspective that always challenges us to ask, "How can I pass this on so that my children will pass it on so they can enjoy the blessings of their heritage in Christ?"

This requires sacrifice, time, hard work, and persevering through our screw-ups as imperfect husbands and fathers. But, is it not God's plan for us, and if so, is not His amazing grace there for us to do it? This is quite different from the American escapist worldview that says, "I raised him/her in a good neighborhood, got him/her a good high school education, and now he/she's finally eighteen, so it's time to cut him/her loose into the world."

We got them through high school, in a nice house. So what? Did we give them core values and a worldview that will last for generations, or are we relieved that they're not our responsibility anymore? When I get to heaven, I don't think Jesus is going to put His arm around me and say, "Son, you were a great preacher—you made people laugh and cry when you presented My Word. Great job!" No, He will look at what I have left behind, and we'll see how well it is doing. The covenant with Abraham was for *all* the generations to follow, and Paul showed us that if we're in Christ, then we're Abraham's heirs. So how did I do passing on the covenant to the generations that follow? Ouch.

Hey, if you have adult children that have fallen away, take heart. Jesus is the covenant keeper. He will listen when we humble ourselves before Him, repent for the non-fathering (our lack), and cry out for mercy. The problem? Men don't humble themselves; therefore, they don't experience renewal in their lives nor in the lives of their descendants. Generational covenant renewal should be a way of life.

Hearkening back to the Mustang, it took tough work to remove the broken or rusted parts to prepare it for renewal. In the same way it takes hard work to address the sinful and dark parts of our children when they are young, to show them how to live with a clear conscience and in a renewed state. If dad does not do this for his children, then no one does. No wonder college students are Marxists today.

As we move on, my hope is that we now begin to look at life, and our own lives, through the lens of this worldview of covenant. It makes life clearer, and it will connect the dots for us as we unpack the man's call as the family gatekeeper.

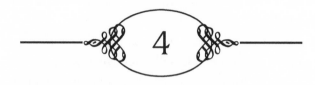

Representation—A Secret Weapon

I stated in chapter 2 that point 2, representation, was probably the most important point to grasp and learn how to apply. Let's take a shot at it now.

Whenever we read about, hear about, talk about, and sing about the good news of the Gospel that Jesus became human and died in our place to pay the price we owed God for our sins, we are declaring and celebrating representation at its very best. The Gospel is the story of representation that provided the atonement for our sins. Consider Paul's instruction to us in Romans 5:

> Therefore, just as sin came into the world through one man, and death through sin, and so death spread to all men because all sinned—for sin indeed was in the world before the law was given, but sin is not counted where there is no law. Yet death reigned from Adam to Moses, even over those whose sinning was not like the transgression of Adam, who was a type of the one who was to come. (vv 12–14)

Notice that before Moses gave the law, men inherited the death sentence from Adam even though they didn't commit the exact same sin. In other words—very important words—Adam represented every human being ever to be conceived and born of men in his sin, and thus, the guilt of his "original sin" is passed to every baby born.

But that's not fair! You're right; take it up with Adam. God didn't eat the fruit. Here is the vast power of representation at work, but it gets so much better:

> If because of one man's trespass, death reigned through that one man, much more will those who receive the free gift of righteousness reign in life through one man Jesus Christ… For as by one man's disobedience the many were made sinners, so by the one man's obedience the many will be made righteous. (Rom. 5:17)

Adam represented you and me in his sin and passed on both guilt and death. Jesus represented you and me on the cross, in His atoning death, and passed on both forgiveness and eternal life. Wow, if I didn't have two knee replacements, I'd stop writing and do a couple backflips to celebrate! Jesus is our representative—He died in our place, just like Adam sinned in our place. In other words, it's as if you and I were standing next to Eve and taking the fruit, and it's like you and I were on that cross getting our sins paid!

The thread continues in the book of Hebrews as the author shows us how the entire Old Testament sacrificial system was based upon covenantal representation:

> For when every commandment of the law had been declared by Moses to all the people, he took the blood of calves and goats, with water and scarlet wool and hyssop, and sprinkled both the book itself and all the people, saying, "This is the blood of the covenant that God commanded for you." (Heb. 9:19–20)

Whose blood did Moses sprinkle on the people and the book of the covenant? He sprinkled the blood of sacrificial animals, chosen as substitutes for "all the people," whose sins were being covered temporarily…until they sinned again, of course. So the people did not pay for their sins with their own lives; rather, the animals represented them. Our author concludes this passage by declaring that "without the shedding of blood there is no forgiveness of sins" (Heb. 9:22).

Some important points stand out in this text. First, God dealt with Adam, Noah, Abram, and now all of Israel, through covenant, as He does with us today, through the Lord Jesus Christ and His complete sacrifice. Covenant is the only way to God. Thus, a covenant worldview is critical to living as effective gatekeepers. Second, the sacrifices offered in the covenants were substitute "representatives" of those who broke/break the covenant. And third, since gatekeepers live by covenant, we must function in an accountable and representative government, to those above us and to those in our charge. There are no exceptions. Single moms need help from the elders and men and women in the local church who are in covenant with them. Can we see the representative principle of covenant deep at work? It changed us at Calvary and now continues as a way of life for the man who wants to be the gatekeeper to his family.

Let's look at a great example of representation at work in everyday life in the New Testament. Matthew 8 and Luke 7 both give us the account of a Roman centurion who had a very sick servant, near death. We need to read the text here to see clearly the main point, so we'll look at both accounts, written by two different men (Matthew and Luke) about the same event:

> When he entered Capernaum, a centurion came forward to him, appealing to him, "Lord, my servant is lying paralyzed at home, suffering terribly." And he said to him, "I will come and heal him." But the centurion replied, "Lord I am not worthy to have you come under my roof, but only say the word, and my servant will be healed." (Matt. 8:5–8)

Now a centurion had a servant who was sick
and at the point of death, who was highly valued by
him. When the centurion heard about Jesus, he sent
to him elders of the Jews, asking him to come and
heal his servant. And when they came to Jesus, they
pleaded with him earnestly, saying, "He is worthy
to have you do this for him, for he loves our nation
and he is the one who built us our synagogue." And
Jesus went with them. When he was not far from
the house, the centurion sent friends, saying to him,
"Lord, do not trouble yourself, for I am not worthy
to have you come under my roof. Therefore I did
not presume to come to you." (Luke 7:2–7)

It is worth noting first that Luke was a physician, and therefore, by profession, a man given to scientific detail, which we see in his gospel and clearly in this story, but also in the depth of his account of the Lord's birth. I doubt there would be a church Christmas program without reading from Luke chapters 1 and 2. Thus, in the centurion's story, Luke tells us that he sent elders to request Jesus's ministry for the sick servant; then, he sends friends to tell him he is not worthy of Jesus's presence in his house.

Matthew, on the other hand, completely eliminates any third party help and tells us that the centurion himself went to Jesus to ask for help. So which guy is telling the truth? Is one of the gospel writers a liar? Is Matthew asleep at the wheel, or perhaps in a hurry that day, so he cuts out the middleman in the story, twice?

No, Matthew gives an accurate account, as does Luke, but Matthew writes the story "representatively"—as if the centurion himself went to Jesus, because he was accurately represented by trusted ambassadors. So, to Matthew, the elders' and friends' words were the centurion's words. It didn't matter that he was not physically present, because he actually was, through those who represented him. This is consistent with covenant representation in the Scriptures, as we saw above in Adam representing us in his sin and Jesus representing us in His payment for the sin.

Here is another great example:

> For though you have countless guides in Christ, you do not have many fathers. For I became your father in Christ Jesus through the gospel. I urge you the, be imitators of me. That is why I sent you Timothy, my beloved and faithful child in the Lord, to remind you of my ways in Christ, as I teach them everywhere in every church. (1 Cor. 4:15–17)

Paul is speaking both generationally and representatively. This is covenant language if there ever was any. As Paul's spiritual son, Timothy is representing "dad" and the family values, as if "dad" were actually there. Paul is not telling them that every time they go off course, Timothy will remind them, "Hey, guys, that's not how Paul wants you to do it." This is, of course, absurd. Rather, he sends Timothy as his representative to teach as he would, to act as he would, and to guide them as he would. Get it? The charge takes on greater authority because Paul speaks of Timothy as his son and of himself as spiritual father to the Corinthian Church.

I stated earlier that Jake is a very good baseball player—better than I ever was, but what I look for is how he represents my worldview as he leads on the field and what values he imparts as opportunities arise. Does he stand strong and calm under pressure? Does he put his teammates first? Does he look to make the coach successful? Does he play with both courage and respect? Does he outwork and outserve and outthink everyone else out there? This is what I have endeavored to instill in him: the "why" he is out there. And when he gets it, he brings success to the team, himself, Christ, and the family name. He may have a good game behind the plate (he's a catcher), but if he isn't constantly outthinking the other guys, his talent will only take him so far. This is representation at work. Don't misunderstand me here—I am not pressuring Jake to live out my unfulfilled dreams in his career. Not at all. I was a centerfielder, and he's a catcher. There's not a lot I can teach him about the mechanics of catching, so he already knows he doesn't need my technical advice. Hence, no pressure.

Also, he knows my love for him, that I'm his biggest fan, and that I'll have his back on a bad day. The bigger issue is that he has the honor of carrying the family name, and our values in Christ, on the field and in the dugout with him. Like Timothy, Jake knows how I would handle a situation, and he factors that insight into his actions. Hey, I've been around a lot longer than my youngest son and have learned more, failed more, repented more, followed Jesus more, seen more, and done more. I am a thief if I don't give him what I have to help him succeed! When Jake thinks as a "son" on his team, his goal is not to take what he can and win that scholarship. Rather, he wants the coach to have a stronger team when he graduates than he has now, because Jake has invested in the "family business." A hireling lives for himself, a son lives for others.

Is this any different, in principle, than Timothy selling out for the Corinthians and making dad's efforts worthwhile by imparting Paul's life values and message to the brethren at Corinth? This wasn't Timothy's first rodeo. He served under Paul and learned the why, what, and how in being a leader and a man from him. He trusted Paul because Paul "sold out" for his spiritual son. Do we "sell out" as dads when our sons and daughters need us most—in everyday life? When we have won their hearts, they will listen to our wisdom and want to represent us, because it will be the way they think! Jake is not out to "please me"; rather, he is out to be the noble man the Lord created him to be. It is my honor and role to show him what that looks and smells like in every aspect of life. Note that I never "delegated" this responsibility to a youth leader or another pastor. He is my son who carries my name, not theirs. Is it challenging and even scary at times? Do I screw up at times? Of course! But...we have Jesus to make us great gatekeepers. Representation is a clear path to get there.

Back to our story of the centurion:

> "Only say the word and my servant will be healed. For I too am a man under authority, with soldiers under me. And I say to one, 'Go', and he

goes, and to another, 'Come', and he comes, and to my servant, 'Do this', and he does it." When Jesus heard this He marveled and said to those who followed him, "Truly, I tell you with no one in Israel have I found such faith." (Matt. 8:8–10)

"But say the word, and let my servant be healed. For I too am a man set under authority, with soldiers under me, and I say to one, 'Go', and he goes; and to another 'Come,' and he comes; and to my servant, 'Do this,', and he does it." When Jesus heard these things, he marveled at him. (Luke 7:7–9)

Well, Matthew and Luke certainly agree upon the centurion's worldview of representation. Notice the centurion does not emphasize his stalwart faith; rather, he explains the basis of his belief: because Jesus is under authority, like he is, all Jesus needs to do is speak from miles away and his servant will be healed.

This humble Roman soldier is teaching us a key representative principle: God does not separate power from authority. Therefore, those that are under proper delegated authority are empowered to act with representative authority, on behalf of those whom they represent. He knew Jesus was under His Father's authority, having been sent to a fallen people, and Jesus therefore carried "authorized power" in His words. The centurion nailed it so well that Jesus marveled. I'm guessing that didn't happen too often. He even implies to the Jews, "Hey, why don't you guys get this?"

This Roman centurion had solid, calm faith because he understood the source of Jesus's power, in His words and His deeds, was legitimate. Jesus carried heaven's authority, not just because He was sent, but also because He had shown Himself to be under His Father's authority. How else would the centurion have been able to claim, "For I *too* am a man under authority." How did he know? Jesus lived representatively, so much so that He made it clear in the gospels that He did what He saw the Father do.

Friend, representation is not a difficult concept to understand, but it's not always easy to embrace and live by, especially in our culture that promotes self-image and self-worth, and "equality" in all situations, at all times…meaning I am free from the perceived oppressive restraints of authority, even if that authority is there to prepare me for destiny. Therefore, we buy the lie and don't impress upon our sons and daughters, when they are young, the miracle of representation and how it can make life simpler and cleaner.

Remember our look at the man's representative place in his family and how the place of appeal, which the covenant guarantees, creates a safe environment and builds trust in the family for their gatekeeper. If you want a healthy family, I don't know of a better way to get it. Now, this doesn't mean we flip a switch and everything is warm and cozy. If we've been messing up for months or years, it will take some time and some humbling and repentance on our parts (more on this later), but Jesus wants to and will redeem our families. This is who He is: Redeemer!

If the King of kings marveled at this discourse, and wisdom, from a foreign soldier, as told by Matthew and Luke, perhaps we also should. Beyond the safety the place for appeal provides, the centurion hit on this key principle in the covenant: God gives governmental authority and power to those He can trust, because they are already accountable. We see this at work in the Corinthian Church, as Paul is bringing the lumber to his spiritual flock for not dealing with the guy getting cozy with his dad's wife (not his mother). We already saw that Paul was sending Timothy to represent him, and now he addresses the sin head on, bringing representative judgment to it, even from another physical location.

> It is actually reported that there is sexual immorality among you, and of a kind that is not tolerated even among pagans, for a man has his father's wife… Let him who has done this thing be removed from among you. For though I am absent in body, I am present in spirit; and as if present, I have already pronounced judgment

> on the one who did such a thing. When you are assembled in the name of the Lord Jesus and my spirit is present with you, with the power of our Lord Jesus, you are to deliver this man to Satan for the destruction of the flesh, so that his spirit may be saved in the day of the Lord. (1 Cor. 5:1–5)

Whoa, brother, who does this guy Paul think he is? Well, in my opinion—and that's all it is, my opinion—this is the most humble man in the early church, after Jesus, of course. He is not "pulling rank" out of pride or to show off. Rather, he is exercising his governmental authority to apply the power that has been entrusted to him by the Most High God. The Lord delegates real power, while men pretend to in an effort to control others. Notice Paul pronounced judgment while not there but "present in spirit," and he would be present with them "in spirit" to apply proper church discipline. Representation comes with power, the real kind of power that changes lives and protects those in need. It was as if he was in Corinth with the brothers.

So let us embrace this core reality and ask ourselves:

> Whom do I represent (i.e., to whom am I accountable)?
>
> Am I in a healthy local church that provides me with strong leadership?
>
> Whom do they represent (i.e., to whom are they accountable)?
>
> If married, is my wife free to rat on me?
>
> Have I won the hearts of my children?
>
> Have I built a safe environment for my family so they might thrive?
>
> Have I represented the covenant to my family on a regular basis?
>
> Have I intentionally taught them a worldview?

A final point about a gatekeeper and his local church—notice I said "his" church—man must have a church where he and his family can serve, and he can be accountable. If I'm a gatekeeper who needs proper representation, how can it exist if I am not submitted to the elders in a local church? The institution of the local church is one of God's governments in a society, and without it, that society is doomed. Paul and Peter had made this clear.

In the era of "buffet Christianity," because of a "Christian humanism" worldview where we make decisions apart from authority, men don't often seek a church or even think about it. Or, in the name of freedom, they have church in their home and are pursuing an organic experience because this is "authentic Christianity," not the institutional church. By the way, I'm not attacking the principle of a legitimate house church. I am pointing out that the disenfranchised and disillusioned have forgotten that safety and power are available to a man under elders' authority.

I don't have time here to address the egalitarian humanism I've heard in many believers over the years who have "thrown off the yoke of religious authority," because some pastor was a jerk. Aren't we all jerks at times? We cannot eliminate or nullify the overt teachings of Scripture on church authority because some people have abused it. I know many, many men who are pastors that have, and will, lay their lives down for the flock. These are great gatekeepers, who should be followed by faithful men, who can then faithfully lead their families.

Take heart, friend. We will now build our case for the man.

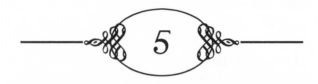

Origins—Who God Really Created the Man to Be

> In the beginning God created the heavens
> and the Earth. The Earth was without form and
> void, and darkness was over the face of the deep.
> And the Spirit of God was hovering over the face
> of the waters. And God said, "Let there be light,"
> and there was light. (Genesis 1:1–3)

Let us establish now that God is God—He is not of this world. He is transcendent above and beyond all things, the sovereign and immortal eternal Creator. He is omnipotent and omniscient and omnipresent, without end, and so on...

The point is this: the Most High God, in His absolute aseity (self-existence), created the world and all that is within it and all universes and galaxies as only He could—"ex nihilo"—from nothing. He spoke, and it was. The end. If we don't ascribe to this, then we'll struggle with the Lord's absolute purpose and plan for the man, especially in our emasculated culture that apologizes for legitimate manhood—a man simply living out his purpose as ordained by his Creator. Such is the approach here, where we don't seek to embellish to impress anyone; rather, we will take an objective look at what the Holy Scriptures declare and let them determine our viewpoint.

> Then God said, "Let us make man in our image, after our likeness. And let them have dominion over the fish of the sea and over the birds of the heavens and over the livestock and over all the Earth and every creeping thing that creeps on the Earth." So God created man in his own image, in the image of God he created him; male and female he created them. (Gen. 1:26–27)

Make note of a few important things. One, only mankind is made in the image of his Creator, and therefore, given a soul. Two, this image puts mankind forever over Creation, as God's representatives. And three, the male and female find their beginnings in the man (see v 27 [emphasis added]: "He created *him*; male and female he created them").

Read on: "And God blessed them. And God said to them, 'Be fruitful and multiply and fill the Earth and subdue it and have dominion over the fish of the sea and over the birds of the heavens and over every living thing that moves on the Earth'" (Gen. 1:28).

Then, notice that men and women were made to procreate, not to resist this call. The man and woman thus had to teach their descendants how to exercise dominion over the creation as God's representatives. The role of the gatekeeper is beginning to show up here—Adam had to initiate this training and ensure it was passed on as it is a generational duty. God did not give contingencies in case mankind didn't like his role. And finally, we must therefore ask, "Did our role change?"

The first chapter of Genesis is Moses's prologue on the account of creation, and in chapter 2, he transitions to a specific narrative on what the creation and determination of man's role looked like: "The Lord God formed the man of dust from the ground and breathed into his nostrils the breath of life, and the man became a living creature. And the Lord God planted a garden in Eden, in the east, and there he put the man whom he had formed" (Gen. 2:7–8).

Only the man was created at this time, supporting Genesis 1:27, and thus, the woman had yet to come into being. God specifically places the man in a garden He created.

He gave man his calling: "The Lord God took the man and put him in the garden of Eden to work it and keep it" (Gen. 2:15). Thus, the man was put in charge of the garden, consistent with divine purpose as stated in chapter 1. The garden needed the man to work it and keep it. It would thus not just produce and keep on its own. The man has his job description, which is the clue to his origin and purpose. And finally, God never rescinded this purpose after the fall.

Many folks describe the garden in Eden as a utopia, in which Adam, with his wife Eve, could run around naked, staying in excellent shape and having great sex while not having any concern about what they would eat or for their safety. The garden would simply provide, like the perfect cartoon. Wrong!

We need to look at these key words, work and keep, to get a clear picture of who we are. We'll use *Strong's Dictionary and Concordance* and the *Bible Dictionary* for our definitions. Then we'll look at where and how these Hebrew words are used in the Old Testament to complete the canvas.

Work—to work (by impl.—serve, till)

Work—bring to pass; cause to happen; husbandman (a farmer)

Are you thinking what I'm thinking? I thought so. Why would Adam have to till the garden? (By the way, where did he buy his tools?) Why would he have to cause the growth of the crops in the garden to happen? Why did he farm the land and not just let it happen—after all, we're talking about Eden here?

Keep—to hedge about (as with thorns)

Keep—to guard, to protect, attend to—beware, be circumspect, take heed

I know, this is crazy, right? Why did Adam have to put a protective hedge around this garden? There, by the way, is a major hint here about man's role as gatekeeper. What were the threats so that he had to be wary of something and be on guard and protect the garden? From what, or whom? Observe the choice of wording in some other translations:

> And the Lord God took the man, and put him into the garden of Eden to dress and keep it. (KJV)

So the Lord God took the man [He had made] and settled him in the Garden of Eden to cultivate and keep it. (AMP)

The Lord God took the man and placed him in the garden of Eden to work it and watch over it. (HCSB)

The Lord God took the man and put him in the Garden of Eden to work it and take care of it. (NIV)

Then the Lord God took the man and put him in the garden of Eden to tend and keep it. (NKJV)

And the Lord took the man and put him in the Garden of Eden to tend and guard and keep it. (AMPC)

Huh, they all are making the same point about Adam's job in the garden—he had to work to provide for, and he had to protect from…

Moses uses the Hebrew word for "work" in Deuteronomy 28, the famous—or "infamous" if you're a covenant-breaker—chapter declaring judgments that would come as a result of the people choosing not to "obey the voice of the Lord your God or be careful to do all his commandment and his statutes that I command you this day, then all these curses shall come upon you and overtake you" (Deut. 28:15). Thus, the context for our word is the Lord causing difficulty, effort, pain, and failure for a rebellious people, so He states in Deuteronomy 28:39 (emphasis added), "You shall plant vineyards and *dress* [work] them, but you shall neither drink of the wine nor gather the grapes, for the worm shall eat them." The Israelites will do what they do—plant a vineyard, and then tend, cultivate, farm, work it so it produces a harvest—but this time it won't yield. The point is that they would work it, just like Adam was told to work the garden.

Now let us see this word *keep* used in other spots in the Old Testament—the same Hebrew word in various places:

> He drove out the man, and at the east of the garden of Eden, he placed the cherubim and a flaming sword that turned every way to *guard* the way to the tree of life. (Gen. 3:24; emphasis added)

> Behold, I am with you and will *keep* you wherever you go, and will bring you back to this land. (Gen. 28: 15; emphasis added)

Here, God is promising to protect Jacob: "I will again pasture your flock and *keep* it" (Gen. 30:31; emphasis added).

Jacob is promising Laban that he would care for and protect the sheep, because sheep don't protect themselves—that's what shepherds do. "The Lord bless you and *keep* you" (Num. 6:24; emphasis added).

This is the beginning of the covenant benediction, calling for God's favor and protection upon His people.

I trust that Lord has made His point here. Adam was in a sinless setting but still had to work, produce, watch, guard, and protect, just as we are to do with our "gardens"—our families—unless of course the Lord changed this later in the Scriptures... He did not.

Chapter 2 of Genesis gives us males clarity on the type of responsibility we are to carry and fulfill in the journey of life. We are by design producers, initiators, makers, providers, guardians, protectors, and defenders; we are the gatekeepers of the family, and the Earth, as He stated in Genesis 1:26–28. We do what He would do, as His image-bearing representatives.

Ponder one more item to confirm this point. Adam had to till, cultivate, and work the garden. I'm just curious about something—where did he get his tools? This is a man who in chapter 2 named the entire animal kingdom, not a primitive cave dweller who grunted and clubbed his way into a more intelligent state over the next million or so years. Rather, he had the God-implanted awareness, intelligence, and skill to design and construct tools for farming, right? That is, unless the Lord created the tools "ex nihilo" or from the raw materials in the Earth. However, this latter view is inconsistent with the context of chapters 1 and 2, in which the man is created for, and charged with, both challenging and complicated tasks.

Here is the point for you and me: the second Adam, the Lord Jesus Christ, restored us through His salvific work, in our minds and souls. Thus, we can fulfill what Adam did not, by faithfully reflecting the image of our Creator though our work (by God's grace working in us), that image restored by the finished work of Christ on the cross. So, if Adam was made to be the gatekeeper, so are we today. Wow.

Representative Authority

> So out of the ground the Lord God formed
> every beast of the field and every bird of the heavens
> and brought them to the man to see what he would
> call them. And whatever the man called every liv-
> ing creature, that was its name. (Gen. 2:19)

God entrusted the man, before the woman was created, with the governmental authority to name, not just an animal but entire species. This confirms God's plan that the human race would rule over all other species. When each of our eight children were born, we didn't ask them, or the nurses, what we ought to name them. We prayed, studied name meanings, discussed, and finally settled on first and middle names for each one, with specific meanings based upon what we believed the Lord was impressing upon us about their respective destinies. Naming is an act of covenant authority. Sadly today, couples are boldly going where no one has gone before in the aimless naming of their children, as now a name that strikes others as authentic, unique, and fashionable is a name for which to be jealous. Often I'll ask the new dad the meaning of his son's name, and he doesn't know. I'm astonished, because this is holy ground for the gatekeeper. How in the world can a man stand in the gate for the next forty to fifty years, if the Lord gives him that long, if he can't even get out of the starting blocks when his children enter life waiting to be named for purpose, and with meaning. "A good name is to be chosen rather than great riches" (Prov. 22:1). Listen, my goal is not to berate young dads who are probably untaught. Hopefully some of you are reading this and it will give you the clues to family destiny, which you can and will lead, because you are made to do so.

Now, while the Scriptures do not give us God's reasoning in not having Eve on hand to help Adam, it is noteworthy that he accomplished the greatest taxonomical feat in the history of creation—alone. I've been waiting for a couple chapters to use that word—pretty cool, eh? Taxonomy is the science of classification, which Adam invented in Genesis chapter 2, while he classified every species on Earth.

So why is it that in so many counseling sessions with couples I'd hear the wife pleading, often with tears, "I just want him to be the spiritual leader of our family. I don't care how much money he makes, or if we drive new cars." I'd then look over at the man and watch his eyes slowly glaze over (most likely, going to his happy place in his mind) and just stare ahead. I recall trying to talk guys into being leaders, gatekeepers. I no longer do marriage counseling and I'm a much happier man for it, and for this simple reason, the guy would not listen; he'd go passive on me and we'd get nowhere. Sometimes he'd let his wife have it when they got home (and I don't mean wild sex), thanks to his haunting insecurity that caused him to fear this serious responsibility.

And yet, how could I blame them? These men were untaught, unprepared, and untrained to "work and keep" the garden known as the family. We all were! It's even worse today, as I observe young and middle-aged dads get pushed around and controlled by their children. I'd really like to see this end, brothers, wouldn't you? Remember, it begins with our worldview and then gets into our intellect and soul—an inside out process. So hang in there. It gets better! We can conclude from the text that the man was totally capable of incredible accomplishments in the fulfilling of his purpose, before his hot wife showed up.

The Cattle and the Beasts

Now, let's consider who man named—every beast of the field, every bird of the air, and all livestock. Genesis chapter 2 makes the same distinction between the livestock and the beasts of the field that we find in the creation account in chapter 1: "And God said, 'Let the Earth bring forth living creatures according to their kinds—livestock and creeping things and beasts of the Earth according to their kinds'" (Gen. 1:24). *Kind* literally means "species." Hence the livestock such as cattle were a different species from the beasts of the field. This is important as events unfold. The livestock were, according to *Strong's Dictionary*, "a dumb beast, especially any large quadruped; cattle." The beast however is a very different story. *Strong's Dictionary* defines beasts as "alive, raw, strong; [wild] beast." Clearly the Lord made two very different classifications of land animals on the sixth day, which brings us to a key point: it is not unreasonable to assume, since the text doesn't clarify overtly, that the wild beasts of the field may have been placed outside the garden. The word *field* in the Hebrew means "spread out; a field [as flat]—country, field, ground, land, soil, wild." Okay, so this field has wildness to it and looks like it's out "in the country," as in a rural, uncultivated setting, often away from populated areas. It's safe to say that God put these "wild" beasts in untamed, uncultivated, "wild" country that spread out beyond the garden. Remember, the Lord had created the entire Earth by this point and not everything was Eden.

Thus we have the cattle and birds in Adam's care and the beasts outside the garden that were, at least, undomesticated. This would explain the responsibility upon Adam to be on guard, to watch, to protect, and to defend. What else would he consider a threat?

Hey, I'm not trying to read into the Holy Scriptures. I fear God too much to do that. I'm just offering a conclusion based upon some deductive reasoning, in light of what the text has shown us. It is entirely possible that Adam had to protect everything in the garden from the "raw, strong, wild" beasts that were outside the garden. I mean, why would the Lord put wild beasts, which would include predators, within the borders of the garden, next to the tasty livestock? This isn't socialism here where every animal is equal in every way. Is this making some sense? Good.

Now we'll see why understanding this distinction is important. There are two conclusions upon which we base our next discovery. One, Adam named every living species in the world. And two, the wild beasts were not the good guys, hence the need for Adam to protect.

The Woman

So, after the man's journey into taxonomy, the Lord makes a woman for him from his rib—we all know this story—not from the dust of the Earth but from the man. Paul expounds upon this in his writings, which we'll see later. The woman is called his "helper," which means "aid; to help, succor; from root—to surround" (*Strong's Dictionary*). Hence, the woman completes her man. The Amplified translation states, "I will make him a helper [one who balances him—a counterpart who is] suitable and complementary for him" (Gen. 2:19). The word *counterpart* literally means "his opposite." The word *complementary* denotes "that which completes." So the wife completes the man, and the husband completes the woman. However, there is no indication that the burden for vigilance, guarding, and protecting falls to the woman. It was specifically given to the man. In fact, as a counterpart, the woman would be capable of and responsible for areas different from the man, opposite him, so that together they complete the picture of fullness of oneness required to raise a healthy family. By the way, the man named the woman, not vice versa. Hence, there is exercise of covenant authority in the marriage.

The Serpent

This leads us to the most tragic event in history—the fall: "Now the serpent was more crafty than any other beast of the field that the Lord God had made" (Gen. 3:1). I'll conclude from that text that one, God made the serpent, since he is classified as a beast of the field. Two, the beasts of the field were not just strong but also were crafty, but the serpent was the craftiest ("most cunning") of them all. And finally, the second point confirms our conclusion about the dangerous nature of the wild beasts of the field.

And now, for the big news: Adam had named the serpent, since he named every beast of the field ("every type"), so he knew something about this guy. He knew the category to which this creature belonged, since he identified it in chapter 2. Thus, he was familiar with its dangerous and deceptive tendencies. If I'm supposed to guard against an enemy, I need to be familiar with his properties and strengths and tendencies, which Adam was, right? In fact, we'll see that this serpent was in some way, the devil, so that should have had Adam running to his gun safe to get locked and loaded.

The word *serpent* used here means "a snake [from its hiss]," which comes from a Hebrew root word "to hiss, i.e., whisper a spell." Thus, this serpent was from the snake family, which Adam had identified and named. If you have ever encountered a poisonous snake, you know how dangerous and stealth-like they can be, just waiting to strike. This serpent was something like this, and this word is used often in the Old Testament referring to the slippery, sneaky reptile.

At the same time, this particular serpent was more, for it in some way represented Satan. John, the Revelator, ties Satan and the serpent together: "And the great dragon was thrown down, that ancient serpent who is called the devil and Satan" (Rev. 12:9). There are a few different views as to this serpent's characteristics, but most Bible scholars agree that the devil possessed it in some way and thus acted through it in the confrontation with Eve. This makes the most sense to me. Let's visit the account:

> He (the serpent) said to the woman, "Did God actually say, 'You shall not eat of any tree in the garden'?" And the woman said to the serpent, "We may eat of the fruit of the trees in the garden, but God said, 'You shall not eat of the fruit of the tree that is in the midst of the garden, neither shall you touch it, lest you die'." But the serpent said to the woman, "You will not surely

die. For God knows that when you eat of it your
eyes will be opened, and you will be like God,
knowing good and evil." So when the woman
saw that the tree was good for food, and that it
was a delight to the eyes, and that the tree was to
be desired to make one wise, she took of the fruit
and ate, and she also gave some to her husband
who was with her, and he ate. (Gen. 3:2–6)

Observe three things. Firstly, the serpent talked. There is no
indication anywhere in Scripture that the animals, birds, et al., that
Adam named had the ability to speak. This should set off an alarm
in Adam's head, right? After all, he was entrusted with the safety of
the garden and all that was in it, including Eve. Secondly, where was
Adam when all this was taking place? He was probably right there
with her!

Commentators offer the following three plausible scenarios as
to what being "with her" meant:

1. He was standing next to her when it all took place.
2. He showed up right after the temptation. Eve then
   explained things, and he accepted the fruit from her hand
   and ate it.
3. He was in the vicinity, close enough to see and know the
   conversation was taking place. Thus, he could be considered to be "with" her, and subsequently accepted the fruit
   from Eve.

When considering the use of the Hebrew word for *with* in the
Old Testament, the first scenario is most likely. Yet, even if it was
option 2, Adam still had to hear the story, buy into the lie, and then
commit the sin with full knowledge of what he was doing. Door
number three is a bit of a stretch.

Thirdly, Satan bypassed the man and went right after the
woman to subvert the created order in which the man is the head and
the keeper of the family. This is played out today in so many ways

and patterns that essentially reject male governance in the home. The common denominator of every scenario is buying into the same lie from the garden to overthrow God's created order. Troubled plantings produce troubled fruit.

However, Adam is 100 percent culpable in every scenario, and as Paul explained in Romans chapter 5, he is the federal head and therefore represented every one of us in his sin. This is how we have all inherited the curse of original sin.

Paul addresses this: "I do not permit a woman to teach or to exercise authority over a man; rather she is to remain quiet. For Adam was formed first, then Eve; and Adam was not deceived, but the woman was deceived and became a transgressor" (1 Tim. 2:12–14). I call these "passover Scriptures," because they are so unpopular or provoking or capable of stirring up trouble that churches "pass over" them. Listen, I'm not arguing for a male-dominated relationship—it should be a covenant partnership, and Paul is not telling us that a woman cannot have a teaching gift. Of course she can—my own wife does. The context shows us that Paul is addressing the woman *trying* to exercise governmental authority over the man—that is a problem, because it essentially flips God's order upside down, and serious problems can occur.

The serpent wisely went after Eve, bypassing the "gatekeeper," who most likely would have given him some trouble. It was unfair to Eve, and the husband's abdication and absence is unfair to so many amazing and godly women today. Some things never change…but they should!

Adam did what so many of us do today when the stuff hits the fan in the home—nothing. He did not step in-between his wife and Satan, with a clear "I'll handle this." He did not protect his wife. He did not confront the evil. He was not the man the Lord God had made him to be. This is the same guy who we saw classify every living species, thereby exercising his authority through naming. This is the same guy that up until now had been keeping watch and protecting the garden. Not anymore.

Listen, if someone broke into your home and threatened your wife and little children, are you going to hide under the bed and let your wife handle the evil perp? Perhaps she could reason with him over tea and cookies. I can't answer for all you men, but if it cost me my life to defend my family, so be it. I'd be with Jesus immediately, and my children would know in their souls that dad loved them with his life, and hopefully my sons would be inspired to do the same for their families.

Amazingly, Adam let the serpent into his house, into his private chamber with his wife, and did not stand between her and disaster. If he had been "keeping" the garden, he must have had some experience with it by this time, don't you think? Even if he did, his passivity conquered him at the worst possible moment.

Remember the worldview is one of covenant, so Adam was God's representative in the covenant to all living beings and therefore carried delegated governmental authority. Recall the centurion who understood the power that representative authority gives to one's words. Therefore, Adam carried authoritative power in his words over the serpent, and yet he didn't use it. He could have told the serpent to "go to hell," and the sneaky deceiver would have had to submit. Alas, it didn't happen and here we are. Let us learn from what Adam did not do—from his sin of omission—that we carry this delegated representative authority on behalf of our wives and children, and the devil has to submit to the man in the gate.

On the other hand, if we leave the gate open and unguarded... This mess inevitably brings to mind the countless times I heard men, again in those painful marriage counseling sessions, say with a straight face, "Well, my wife is the spiritual one, because she's just naturally more sensitive to things than I am. That's how women are wired. I can't help it that she can hear spiritual things better than I can." Let me say this about that—what a crock. Since when did the Scriptures inform us that the man is an idiot, incapable of finding God's will for himself and his family in the Holy Scriptures?

However, in truth, guys, Adam did completely blow it, so we're in good company. However again, another "Adam" came to Earth to free us from the bondage we inherited from the first Adam. Why do we still act like we're standing next to Eve while she cozies up to the devil? I repeat, again to encourage us, most of us had clueless training as boys about who and what a man really is and how to live by grace in the image of God. Let's press on.

One can extrapolate from the man's abdication in the garden how simple and reasonable it seems to let our pastors and youth leaders impart the core values of covenant in Christ to our sons and daughters. Hopefully along the way, a coach or mentor will intersect their lives to train them in leadership. Hey, these are great people dedicated to Jesus and serving his people. They simply have not been injected with the spiritual DNA to be gatekeeper to our children. Only we husbands and dads have been given that injection. Time to give thanks to an amazing Creator, guys. How He has blessed us!

When my boys were young, I repeatedly told them they were called to lead with servants' hearts wherever the Lord placed them in life. My explanation was simply that a real gatekeeper must know how to lead. I include my three sons-in-law in this as they are sons to me.

My second son, Bear, is probably the most naturally gifted leader of the group. He has a killer sense of humor, is quick on his feet, can communicate in just about any situation, and is naturally great with people. God gave all this to him. I've told him it's his responsibility to steward it and grow it.

This is where his hard work comes in. He's an avid reader, so I fed him historical book series, core theology material, challenging books on manhood and thinking, and so on. Bear now needs no reading guidance from me as he sends me a great reading. However, we would delve into the core lessons of a book or series and how it linked to our worldview and its relevance in life around us.

Bear is also a gym rat like me (actually he's much better than I was/am), so I started taking him to the gym in his early teens. He was pumping iron with adult men, some of whom were beasts; and the thrill of the lift captured him and he has worked on the created trifecta of body, mind, and spirit. He now passes it on to his children.

This son of mine commands a room when he enters partly due to his gifts but also because he cares about serving those in need. So I recently told him that God wants this ability and heart in him to shine wherever he goes. Thus, he needs to be intentional about capitalizing on opportunities a situation offers to impart courage and life to others. I know he'll do it because I know his heart. He's a great man.

The best news is he doesn't do it alone. Bear and Hannah, my daughter-in-law, not only love each other but also like each other. And they team up in their business endeavors, focusing on what each does best. Hannah can build, and Bear can gather—a great team. They are now investing what is in them in many others.

Here's the bottom line for me with Bear. My responsibility was to see what was in his soul as a young boy and look for ways to water his giftings and his bents in life (not all of my sons love the gym like Bear and I do, so I accounted for that with each of them).

In other words, as the gatekeeper, I invaded Bear's life with whatever wisdom, training, and manly courage I could impart. He took it from there. The gatekeeper is the initiator. We don't wait for a teacher, coach, or youth leader to do it.

The Man's Big Problem
from the Fall

The cosmic disaster known as the fall, in which the man and woman ate of the fruit of the tree of the knowledge of good and evil, brought bondage and curses that work through the generations. There is only one way to conquer the curse, and the Scriptures lead us to it, thanks be to the Most High. Let's look at the "fruit" of this mess.

First—The Actual Sin Adam and Eve Committed

The first and actual sin Adam and Eve committed is one we all battle. This was the sin of autonomy, as the serpent told them, "You will be like God, knowing good and evil" (Gen. 3:5). We spoke earlier of this tendency in the human race, since the beginning, whereby we need to be our own bosses, overthrow proper and delegated authority, and live by our own rules. There truly is nothing new under the sun, for every century has witnessed this debacle. It's really the failed exercise of humanism in which man is at the center. That's right, Adam and Eve invented humanism—the centrality of "me"—and all philosophies since are geared toward discovering, defining, and explaining "Who is 'me'?" The Egyptians, Persians, Greeks, Romans, and most religious sects apart from Christ have taken their shots at it. This of course includes the nineteenth and twentieth-century atheist psychologists.

Actually, a humanist worldview is rather convenient, because we can make up our belief structure, including the invention of our gods, made in human image of course. We can do this because we are at the center—the religion of "me." It's taken on various forms over the centuries, but the core premise is the same—we are central to our evolution, and mankind is inherently good. This point is critical to the serpent's ongoing deception of the human race, since if we buy into our own moral goodness, we can be trusted to come up with the solutions. By the way, if you want to know how this is working out, take a look at our college campuses, which in such an enlightened era, produces graduates that are devoid of a self-conscious worldview and the historic implications of such. Our default Marxist college alumni don't even realize they are overthrowing the brilliant logic of Scripture in our sociopolitical and economic viewpoints. If it continues unchecked, we will become an armpit of the world's failed societies.

This is what Adam and Eve essentially started. I'm guessing they didn't see all this coming but is not every coup, tyrant, dictator, state-controlled society, and impoverished nation in history the result of mankind doing what he wants to others, for the sake of power, money, and fame? I'm still looking for that moral goodness everyone talks about. The core worldview of humanism came to be in Eden and has bred every man-centered view since, for if one's view is not subservient to the Scriptures, then it has another source—man.

Consider the reasoning behind the "isms" most imposed upon peoples today—socialism, Marxism, and communism. In every case, the argument follows this line of thought: "We the people" are being oppressed by some privileged elite class that uses us to achieve their own ends, their wealth, and their power. Thus, the "people" must stand together against such injustice and somehow remove them from their towers of power. Of course, the great irony in America today is that these wealthy "oppressors'" are the people who built the colleges and universities, investing billions in the process. Now these very institutions of learning are promoting the overthrow of their providers. Not too smart, but very serpent-like in its deception. If "we the people" represent the future and as big business and elitists are removed, then "we" then step in and save the day… Because in this case, the "we" is the state, since the logic is that the people are the state. So big brother gets bigger as we feed it by looking to it for protection and provision. After all, if we're inherently good, then the civil government will serve us, because it is us. At least this is the con being sold across the land today.

It is so cunning in its deceptive nature that it's almost brilliant in its sparkling, but false, attraction. Lenin sold the Russian peasants the same lies after the 1917 revolution. They were told that they, the people, were the state, and this movement was about them and for them. It's the same today on American soil. The faces of the leaders have changed, but the lie remains the same—all because Adam chose himself over the will of his sovereign Creator and God.

Thus, we again see the importance of a worldview based upon covenant with God through the Lord Jesus Christ, in which we relate to one another via safe representative authority in that covenant. Men are thus empowered to function as keepers of their own gardens and are accountable for its success. Real representative power is decentralized and runs through the family first. The man applies God's government and prepares the next generation to replace him when the time is right, thus providing succession and continuity in the covenant, as family members spread throughout the society and take their respective places in the various spheres to which God has called them.

Let me share an example with you. Just before writing this section, I sat with my youngest and had a talk with him about the importance of awareness that a man must practice in every situation God places him, so he knows how to act and serve proactively, not out of reaction. Leaders act, while followers react. This came up because of a situation this evening in our home, so I simply capitalized upon it to both teach and train him again about this principle. I didn't criticize him, but I did critique his actions in said situation and used it as an object lesson to make him a better leader than he was before today began.

This happened in the home, not the school or church or the mall. It's who I am, made in the image of God, to impart life to my sons and daughters. It doesn't mean I'm smarter or better than any-one else; rather, I am more empowered by the Lord than anyone else, with full access to His grace and wisdom to "work, till and cultivate" *my garden* because He gave me these children. This is a covenant worldview at work—quite different than the centralized models cited above, based upon mankind's limited wisdom, that rely on "we" to take care of things. No, thanks.

Second—Adam's Fatal Response to Sin that We Forever Will Battle

"Then the eyes of both were opened, and they knew that they were naked. And they sowed fig leaves together and made themselves loincloths" (Gen. 3:7).

Well, Adam is finally taking some initiative, eh? Sadly it's the fruit of the guilt and condemnation that sin brings us—I call it "fig-leafing." The man and the woman covered themselves to hide their naked, sinful state. In other words, they tried to "cover" their tracks, so to speak, and thus justify their actions. Over thirty years as a pastor taught me that men are expert fig-leafers, and the following verses show us why: "And they heard the sound of the Lord God walking in the garden in the cool of the day, and the man and his wife hid themselves from the presence of the Lord God among the trees of the garden" (Gen. 3:8).

Have you ever noticed how sin makes us stupid? I mean, seri-ously, Adam had a fellowship with the Creator that we cannot com-prehend, and saw things we don't see. Yet his strategy, when the Lord showed up, was to hide? As if the Omniscient One would not find them? When we men hide our sin, we close the spout of divine wis-dom and awareness, and run from grace. We become, at best, inef-fective in the gate and usually useless because we're so busy covering ourselves that we can't and don't think of how to cover our families.

"But the Lord God called to the man and said to him, 'Where are you?' And he said, 'I heard the sound of you in the garden, and I was afraid, because I was naked, and I hid myself'" (Gen. 3:9–10). So what do all the Adams of the world do when caught in the shame of sin? We hide, of course. Not from the sin, but from the "sin remover," because of that great paralyzer called shame. It was different before the fall—there was no shame. "Therefore a man shall leave his father and mother and hold fast to his wife, and they shall become one flesh. And the man and his wife were both naked and were not ashamed" (Gen. 2:24–25).

The most profound expression of covenant on Earth is a marriage of a man to a woman, who enter into a oneness that binds them body, mind, and spirit to each other. In our married life, I've been a bit of a gym-rat. I love to work out for a number of reasons. My wife, however, does not. Yet she'll get theological with me after I have a good workout, by explaining that since we're one, when I work out, she's working out. Talk about oneness. Anyway, in this sinless oneness the man and the woman never experienced guilt or shame that follows it, because in their naked state, they were covered by the Lord's justification of them. Recall how after the fall Adam and Eve covered themselves with fig leaves—they had lost their innocent and pure standing before God that His justification provided for them. Nakedness in Old Testament usage presents a picture of humiliation or shame, of weakness and need, all tied to man's guilt before God. He has lost his innocent standing and lives in a state of legal guilt and therefore condemnation before his Maker. Counseling and therapy cannot legally remove the state of guilt from a human being's soul. In fact, most attempts of counseling are doomed if they don't recognize the state of total depravity of the soul which puts him/her at enmity with God every second of every day. You'll find out about more on this later. So, as long as Adam and Eve kept the covenant, they were covered and free from shame, because they were declared just before God, because they were in a sinless state before they fell. Sadly this was short-lived.

After the fall, "Then the eyes of both were opened, and they knew that they were naked. And they sewed fig leaves together and made themselves loincloths" (Gen. 3:7). "Naked" in chapter 2 and then in chapter 3 are two different Hebrew words, with essentially the same meaning, and both words are from the same Hebrew root word. In Genesis 2:25, *naked* means "nude, either partially or totally naked." In Genesis 3:7,10,11, *naked* means "nudity, nakedness." However, chapter 3's usage represents nakedness as in a state of guilt, with the resulting shame. From that point forward, mankind lives in a constant state of shameful awareness of sinfulness, which breeds hiding and self-justification.

How many times have you or I been caught in a potentially damaging situation, and we lie our way out of it or make ridiculous excuses in a feeble attempt to cover our guilt. Can we now see how shame is a man's poison that paralyzes? How can I function as a warrior, defender, and shepherd when I can't get past my own condemnations? I'm talking about redeemed Christian men, whose sins have been forgiven, and to whom Jesus has imputed His righteousness. Thus, we are in a legal, impervious, and impenetrable state of acceptance before the Father, just as Adam was before he sinned. Yet we run from self-examination and don't therefore deal with our ongoing sins that so easily beset us, as the Scriptures state. A dad in the gate teaches and shows his sons and daughters how to self-examine and then confront their hidden sins to find forgiveness and cleansing in Christ and restoration of a clear conscience. This is where all mental health begins. This gives us what Adam had before he fell to sin—he was naked and not ashamed, because he was innocent. Now, just as Adam feared being found out, we hide in our sinful guilt and shame from the Lord, and make excuses—fig leaves. No wonder so many husbands in our culture do not, and cannot, take responsibility for a marriage and family. They can't take responsibility for themselves—their own souls and conscience and relationship with their Father.

Let's consider shame's kidnapping of the conscience and the problems it causes in an individual, a marriage, a family, and ultimately, in society. As I write this, we are living in Southern California for part of the year, and in Upstate New York for the remainder, where in both places I have the privilege of serving pastors and leadership teams in various churches.

Sandra and I share a house with our daughter Luissa and our son-in-law Jon. They have a little Spaniel they named Tesla. Now they can tell their friends they own a Tesla. "Tes" is a great dog, happy and very engaging with people, so we all enjoy her. Tes has one problem—she will when the mood suits her take a dump on the hardwood floor in the living room. Once the evidence is discovered, either Sandra, Luissa, or Jon will call her into the living room to stand trial, be convicted, and sentenced to a proper punishment. Tes is now on to them, and when called, she quietly walks into her sleeping area, as if she's going to take a nap. If they can get her out of there, they will give her a good canine scolding. Her huge ears will go slightly back as she takes the heat. Once finished, there is absolutely no sign of remorse or regret in her being, and we all know she'll do it again soon. She starts running around and the tail gets wagging, as if she never did a thing wrong—because in her soulless mind, she is totally innocent. You see, Tes does not have the equivalent of a human conscience, which has a built-in conviction-meter that goes off when we sin, because that conscience is made in God's image and is designed to go into alarm mode when sin is committed. The conscience is at that point in an unresolved state of guilt, and shame appears as the fruit of that guilt.

When unresolved guilt or shame occurs, it is a warning sign and an indicator of the fork in the road we face every time this happens—we either run to the Lord, because we are already hidden in Christ, where we confess and receive forgiveness and the cleansing of the conscience. This gives us a clear soul and mind free of any guilt, and shame has no power to darken our souls; our relationship with and access to the Father is completely unhindered and we can abide in His life-changing presence every minute. We can freely defend the gate because our spiritual eyesight is 20-20 to allow us to identify any dangers.

Conversely, when we run from the Lord and hide in our nakedness, guilt from sin, we cannot resolve the sense of guilt within, and we must cover up to justify it and compensate for our sense of worthlessness. In reality, God doesn't see us that way—He sees Christ's righteousness in us—but the shame blinds us to reality, and our insecurity goes crazy trying to self-justify. We fear being found out so we use anger, withdrawal, neglect, abuse, mockery, cruelty, perfectionism, criticism, etc., to shift attention and responsibility to others, like a drug to ease the torment. The usual targets are the wives and children, because they are there, without an escape hatch.

We forget about the governmental power of our words and actions as God's covenant representatives—as gatekeepers—and we do more damage in the spiritual and emotional realm than we can imagine. It's a "Wow, he doesn't know his own strength" problem. We are using the power of the covenant in a destructive way, and we leave the house for work, unresolved in conscience and unreconciled to our "sheep." I'm guessing that if we were truly aware of the damage such a wrong use of covenant power causes to those in our care, we'd be on our knees more, asking the Lord for forgiveness first and then for grace to love and lead beside still waters that restores the soul. But an unresolved conscience is a blind conscience, and the shame causes the darkness to get darker and the heart to get harder. The bottom line is, we are covenant-breakers when we fig-leaf. Only God can cover sin and therefore bring covenant renewal to reinstate us in the gate with health in our mind and joy in our souls. I know this is real because the Lord has graciously forgiven me every time I have screwed up and run to Him for forgiveness and renewal.

A renewed man is a man able and willing to work and keep his garden. We are not like Tesla, who can do wrong things and not be fazed, not be malicious or uptight in the process, who has no guilt to hide, and just freely move on in life. Tes is not a fig-leafer because she knows no sense of guilt. Our sense of guilt is really a gift from God, because it is designed to lead us to Him, not to the fig leaf tree.

Friends, shame is the devil's great helper, and we grease the skids for him because of our own insecurities. This is why Paul teaches us to examine ourselves before taking the Lord's Supper, which is an act of covenant renewal (1 Cor. 11:27–31). This is why James tells us to "confess our sins to one another, that we may be healed" (James 5:16). Notice he tells us we'll be healed, not just forgiven. The Lord Jesus gives us the remedy for shame, but shame keeps us from the remedy! Can you relate?

Third—The Massive Problem Man Inherited from the Curse

Well, guys, if you think guilt and its friend shame were a problem for us, now we discover the greatest battle we will face that would keep us from being effective gatekeepers. Remember the apostle Paul's analysis of why things happened the way they did in the fall, and the conclusion he draws from it: "I do not permit a woman to teach or to exercise authority over a man; rather she is to remain quiet. For Adam was formed first, then Eve; and Adam was not deceived, but the woman was deceived and became a transgressor" (1 Tim. 2:12–14). Paul is not saying the man was not deceived but rather that the woman led the way in debating the devil over doctrine that God had established. This was Adam's responsibility as gatekeeper, as we saw above. Eve took the bait and Adam's passivity allowed it to happen. In this regard, the serpent did not directly deceive Adam, but Eve, and then Adam gave in.

Also, the phrase used by Paul "exercise authority over" is the only time it is used in the New Testament, as in the context he is addressing the proper use of governing authority. Chapter 3 immediately follows, which begins with Paul describing the qualifications for an elder in the church, who is to carry oversight or governing authority. The word overseer and elder are used interchangeably in the New Testament, and Paul only includes males as eligible for this governing office. In fact, he makes it clear if the wife and children are in submission that he is an effective leader of the home and therefore qualified to lead a church. If I can't govern my family, I can't govern well outside the home. Thus, he is using the logic in chapter 2 that the woman was deceived and should not govern over the man to support his case for men only being elders. By the way, if this is offensive, it's not my motive. This is what the Holy Scriptures state. God inspired Paul to write this, not me. It is we who have trashed this in exchange for a modern, emasculated gospel that seeks to explain this away, so women can govern men.

Paul further explained his thinking to the church in Corinth when the issue of who should wear a head covering during worship came up. This was a typical pattern in the first century church. The discussion then develops around the issue of spiritual covering, exercising authority, between and man and a woman:

> For a man ought not to cover his head, since
> he is the image and glory of God, but woman is
> the glory of the man. For man was not made from
> woman, but woman from man. Neither was man
> created for woman, but woman for man. That is
> why a wife ought to have a symbol of authority
> on her head. (1 Cor. 11:7–10)

Remember our study earlier on the woman complementing the man? Paul is not demeaning the woman's importance but clarifying the created order for the exercise of authority in the family. He nowhere diminishes the woman's importance. Thus a wife needed a "symbol" of authority. At that time, a head covering was a material sign of such a thing. Today, it is simply the marriage functioning in biblical order. Has the principle of representative authority been changed in the New Testament? Not only has it not been changed but Paul reinforces it.

This is the painful truth we have learned thus far. The woman was deceived, not the man. The man abdicated and left the woman uncovered, so what should have been a safe place for the woman became a death zone. The woman took the lead, because there are no vacuums. And sin corrupted the created order, turning it upside down. Now, let's look at the curse and the ensuing disaster as God addresses the woman—this is at the core of why Paul addressed authority in the home in these epistles. Sin opens the door for a curse: "To the woman He said, 'I will surely multiply your pain in childbearing; in pain you shall bring forth children. Your desire shall be for your husband, and he shall rule over you" (Gen. 3:16). Okay, that sounds good to me—my wife is going to desire me. How is that a bad thing? In fact, she'll be cursed with this desire, so it's not going away. Great, bring it on! Easy fella. Let's take a look at this word *desire* in the Hebrew for clarity. *Desire* is "teshookaw," "a stretching out after; in the original sense, it means to run after or over; overflow [as water overflows]." Wait a minute. My wife is going to want to run over me, flow over me like a stream or river? That's not a good idea! Don't worry, it gets worse.

Let's look at the word usage of "teshookaw" in the Old Testament. It is only used one other time, and its meaning does not sound good for the guys. It occurs in the next chapter of Genesis, after Cain gets angry at and jealous of Abel when they presented their sacrifices to God. Cain's heart wasn't right so the Lord confronts and warns him: "The Lord said to Cain, 'Why are you angry, and why has your face fallen? If you do well, will you not be accepted? And if you do not do well, sin is crouching at the door. Its *desire* is for you, but you must rule over it" (Gen. 4:6–7; emphasis added). Every study Bible I own shows one word as a literal substitute for the preposition *for* in both 3:16 and 4:17, and that is the word *against*. Thus we get "Your desire will be against your husband" to Eve and "Sin's desire will be against you" to Cain. This is aggressive phrasing that pictures the curse manifesting in a desire to oppose and run over or essentially conquer. Further, because the very nature of sin is to conquer and destroy, I don't think the Lord is telling Cain that sin wants to cozy up nice to him because of its warm desire to love on Cain. No, He's warning him that sin is at the doorstep, and it wants to run over and rule him, but Cain is supposed to conquer this sin and do the ruling.

Now let's look at the last line of 3:16, and we find the same wording in the final line of 4:7. In 3:16 (emphasis added), it reads, "And he [the husband] shall *rule* over you [the wife]." In 4:7 (emphasis added), it reads, "But you [Cain] must *rule* over it [sin]." In Hebrew, "rule" is "mashal," which means "to rule; have, make to have, dominion, governor, have power." As with "teshookaw," we must see how "mashal" is used in other Old Testament scriptures to get a more complete picture of its meaning:

> Then the men of Israel said to Gideon, *rule*
> over us, you and your son and your grandson.
> (Judg. 8:22; emphasis added).

The hand of the diligent will *rule*, while the slothful will be put to forced labor. (Prov. 12:24; emphasis added)

Then a mighty king shall arise, who shall *rule* with great dominion and do as he wills. (Dan. 11:3; emphasis added)

The context of these passages clearly show that ruling is the exercise of governmental authority and power over others. In fact, Daniel is prophesying about the rise of Alexander the Great and his reign. It's hard to get any more human dominion or power than Alexander had. So the Lord is telling the woman that the man's place is not to just stop her from running over him but rather to take the mantle of leadership and function with delegated authority and thus use his power to defend his marriage and family. I repeat: man's place is to take the mantle of leadership and function with delegated authority and thus use his power to defend his marriage and family.

Let's put "teshookaw" and "mashal" together in a literal insertion in the text. We get this: "You will be cursed with a desire to oppose and run over your husband, but he shall have power to govern and rule over you" (Gen. 3:16). And "[Sin's] desire will be to oppose and run over you, but you must make sure you have dominion over it and rule it" (Gen. 4:7). Now do we get the picture of the curse that husbands and wives have inherited in every marriage since the fall? The woman is cursed with an addictive desire to overrun her husband, to stand against his leadership, and the husband has no choice but to exercise governing power over her in spite of her desire to be boss.

What a mess, and yet it confirms what we saw as Adam's designated purpose to work and protect his garden. He was designed by God with the inherent properties in his soul and mind to do the job, to be the gatekeeper. This is confirmed by the Lord in the curse planted on the woman in Genesis 3:16, but now it will happen with resistance, both from the wife and hell's agents; however, they, too, can help to make her successful in her coup.

I realize this sounds really out of step with modern Christian philosophy, but again, these are the teachings of Scripture. They are not my words, and they have not changed. This gives clarity to Paul's challenge to husbands and wives in Ephesians 5, in which he tells men to love their wives sacrificially, as Christ did, because it's the only way to *stay* in the gate. Then he tells the women to submit to their husbands, because women's internal battle is to *overrun* the gate. That said, if the husband is abdicating and leaving the gate unprotected against their enemies, she has to step in. However, this is not God's plan.

Recall that Paul wrote about the man being the image and glory of God, while the woman is the glory of the man in 1 Corinthians 11. This is significant because we're seeing the purpose for the image of God in the man: to bring glory to his Creator, according to His design. The prophet Isaiah takes no prisoners in declaring the Lord's holy jealousy for His glory: "I am the Lord; that is my name; my glory I give to no other, nor my praise to carved idols" (Isa. 42:8).

Our ultimate purpose is to glorify our God as we reflect His image in us by living out our purpose according to His design, which He made clear in Genesis 2 and 3, as we have seen. Therefore, we come to this stark conclusion, strictly based upon what we have learned from Scripture. God is not glorified when the reflection of His image through His intended order is corrupted or reversed. Specifically concerning marriage, when a woman governs or leads a man, God does not receive glory. This does not reflect God's order for things. It doesn't matter that things are upside down today, because of the fig-leafing of the man, and the teshookawing of the woman. It is not what God created it to be, and in fact, if God determines this to be a result of the curse, how can it bring Him glory?

I realize many marriages are far from this divine intended order, and in the name of survival, many Christian women see leadership as coequal and also strive to find their ministry purpose in other segments of the culture. However, this does not put the marriage in proper order nor bring the favor of the Most High upon the family as it flows in peace when under godly, sacrificial government.

The good news is that the remedy is in Jesus, but we already see how guilt and shame keep us from the gate, which opens the door for the Mrs. to step right in. And you know what? She will do it because "teshookaw" has been planted in her soul, and she'll get the job done when hubby loses his way. How many amazing single mothers are right now fighting the good fight to raise their children while working full-time, not only without a dad but with the burned-over wounds in her and her children from the guy wimping out and throwing them to the wolves by leaving the gate. I wish some guys would have listened to me over the years and stayed single. By the way, this is not an opposition to women working outside the home. That decision is between husband and wife, but the man is responsible to guide the way and ensure it honors the Creator.

I realize I'm highly biased toward my own children as imperfect as they all are; but my oldest daughter, Lindsay Ruth (I call her Ruthie), is a solid example of confronting the curse of "teshookaw." She and Ben have three children as I write this.

Ruthie was the easiest of our eight to raise; she was quiet (unlike everyone else), a bit shy with a bent toward mercy, stayed to herself, and helped her mom with the young ones. What a blessing. During her twenties, she had an opportunity that awakened the strength within her. A friend of ours was a professional hockey player who, late in his career, signed with a team in Switzerland. He and his wife hired Ruthie to move to Switzerland as an au pair for their three boys. That time away on her own challenged and stretched her.

Then Ben came along, won all of us, and they were married. Ben never met an adventure he didn't like, works hard, loves a good party, and loves his family most. The "new" Ruthie doesn't put up with a lot of nonsense. I have to be careful what wild stories I tell my grandchildren and the sarcastic spin I put on it, or my daughter will shut me down. So she and Ben began to work on finding oneness in their relationship in the face of many differences between them. She takes strong stands on things that matter, and Ben listens to her because she has won his respect as she supports him in his ventures as long as he'll man up in the home.

They aren't perfect, but they are true soulmates who have conquered the curse and live in harmony, each giving the other room to be who he/she is. She doesn't nag to conform him into her image, and he doesn't pretend she carries no power.

Paul struggled with sin in his flesh as he describes in Romans 7:15–18:

> I do not understand my own actions. For I do not do what I want, but I do the very thing I hate. Now if I do what I do not want, I agree with the law, that it is good. So now it is no longer I who do it, but sin that dwells within me. For I know that nothing good dwells in me, that it, in my flesh.

The flesh is our old patterns of sinful behavior, and every family has their inherited negative traits from the previous generations. Paul is explaining a little about his battle with the old tendencies that must be conquered through the power of Christ over time. If a man wants to be a gatekeeper, he must conquer this or get "teshookawed" by his bride, and the real kicker is that it's our fault, not hers. Remember the governmental power Adam carried and could have exercised over the serpent but didn't? That is what we carry and what we should *not* do. Rather, in Christ, we can win the battle and the hearts of our wives and children. Stay tuned.

As we approach the finish line in this section, it behooves us to see what the Lord said to Adam in pronouncing His covenantal sanctions on the man for what he did: "And to Adam he said, 'Because you have listened to the voice of your wife and have eaten of the tree of which I commanded you, 'You shall not eat of it', cursed is the ground because of you; in pain you shall eat of it all the days of your life...'" (Gen. 3:17). Before we run off and build our man caves and buy that '62 Corvette because we no longer have to listen to our wives, I'm guessing the Lord is not making a rule from this curse. Obviously in the context, He's letting Adam "have it" for not standing up to the serpent, who deceived his wife in front of him, and then, for accepting the forbidden fruit from her. The text suggests that Eve spoke to Adam about the desires of the fruit, and he listened, took the bait, and the rest is history.

The Scriptures teach us about the sanctity of oneness in the marriage covenant, in which both spouses bring their insight and wisdom to the table, plus it teaches us how to use that insight. A man who ignores his wife's wise input is a fool indeed. Many times my wife had key input in a situation that required decision and then action. Usually I listen, but sometimes I don't. She knows at that point I'll take responsibility for the final decision. If my decision to ignore her is the wrong one, she never gives me the childish "I told you so." Rather, she gives me the room to work through it, go to the Lord, and make whatever it is right. If my decision was the right one, I don't keep score over her, we just continue to work as a team.

Here's a classic example from our marriage. In 1987, our home church sent my family and me to Northern New York, where I would serve a number of churches across the northern border. Over the months, I built wonderful relationships with the various churches, the pastors, and their elder teams. One church did not have a pastor, and they eventually asked me if I would take the position. I sought the counsel of my oversight back home, and it seemed right at the time. Only one person struggled with it. You guessed it—my soul mate. Being the incredible teammate she was, she chose to faithfully follow me and chalked up her "uncomfortable intuition" to the fact that we would be far from what had been home, something neither of us liked…but it was "for the kingdom." I'd often find her in tears at the end of the day, and I prayed every prayer I knew. I then left on an extended ministry trip, during which I got really sick and every day got up off the canvas to do the meetings and then fell back in bed. It got so bad that I sought the counsel of the two older and more seasoned men with whom I was teaming in the meetings. These are men I had known and respected for years. The consensus was that the Lord was trying to tell me something and was using the illness to get through, because I had not heard Him so far. That night I cried out to the Lord and by His grace decided to not take the pastor's position. I looked forward to informing my wife. The only hitch was that we had a signed offer on a house we were buying in the area and had paid our down payment.

Well, I got home late, about 2:00 a.m. after a long trip back home, told Sandra, and she wept for joy and then she laughed. Two other rather amazing things then happened—the illness quickly went away and the homeowner let us out of the contract and gave us back our money. What's the moral of the story? Unless it's sin, pay attention to the woman who loves you and man up to your decisions, right or wrong.

Now, there is another instance in Scripture in which a key patriarch listened to his wife's words about what she thought he should do. That was in violation of God's plan for them:

> Now Sarai, Abram's wife, had borne him no children. She had a female Egyptian servant whose name was Hagar. And Sarai said to Abram, "Behold now, the Lord has prevented me from bearing children. Go in to my servant; it may be that I shall obtain children by her." And Abram listened to the voice of Sarai. (Gen. 16:1–2)

Well, of course, he listened, right, guys? What a great idea—my wife actually wants me to have sex with another woman; in fact, it's her idea! Whoa, boys. Again, the context is that God has promised Abram a son through the covenant He initiated with the man, and his wife had still not conceived. She was beyond childbearing years, so she comes up with her own plan to help the Lord's plan come to pass. As with Adam, we read this and think, "Hey, buddy, are you crazy? Hasn't God done some amazing things already on your behalf, like allowing Abram to rescue Lot from an army that captured him, with just 318 men?" Yes, He has, and yet Abram heeded Sarai's "wisdom" in a major directional decision.

Remember Paul told us that Eve was deceived; such is the case here as well. Sarai became deceived and then posed a seemingly crazy option for Abram to take, and, like Adam, he took it. In both cases disaster was the result; Ishmael, who was born to Abram and Hagar, became the father of those who follow Islam in the Middle East. How did that work out? The point is, that the man has the prime responsibility to guard against all error and falsehood in the family, and to guide his wife and family beside still waters and green pastures. Both Adam and Abram abandoned the gate, and Eve and Sarai were left to the mercy of their enemies.

What can we conclude from this mess? The responsibility to lead is left to the man, and the woman wants to boss him around, or at least fix him, while the man wants to avoid responsibility. The man will "fig leaf" when he fails, but eventually his autonomy kicks in and he redefines manhood. Her issue is relational, while his issue is tied to who he is…identity. There are no vacuums—someone will always govern. But when the man abandons the gate, his enemies are waiting for his family. However, the man was made to lead, and Jesus came to restore him. His godly government provides a safe place for his wife and children to be themselves and prosper.

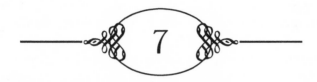

The Man as Gatekeeper—A Picture Painted

First—Understand the Governments of God

Firstly, it's imperative to understand the governments of God. While traveling to a meeting today, I had the radio tuned to a talk radio host that I respect. He was discussing the philosophical battle in our culture between those who prefer a welfare state to care for them and those who ascribe to personal liberties and responsibilities. In case you haven't figured it out yet, I'm on the second team because of my covenant worldview. Every time he referred to the actions of the "state" (i.e., local, state, or federal magistrates and legislators), he called it the "government," as in "the government wants to limit individual freedoms so people become more dependent on the government for their futures." I know that by "government" he means the civil jurisdiction in society, not the family or private sector, or the church. However, the word *government* has, over time, come to mean only the elected politicians and civil branch of society that makes laws, executes them, and tries the offenders of those laws. Yet that is not at all what our forebears saw or wanted. Rather they taught the principle of self-government, which would produce healthy families, which would provide the three main spheres of corporate society: church, civil, and commercial government, with productive leaders and producers. A government referred to whichever sphere of society was the topic.

Therefore the governments of God in a healthy society are self-government in which a man breeds healthy…family government which prepares the children for roles in… church, civil, and commercial (i.e., the marketplace) governments. Each government, per our definition used earlier, is "a sphere in society properly governed by delegated authority, all of which comprise the governments that function within prescribed jurisdictions." In other words, each "government" is responsible for its jurisdiction and is not allowed to overrun and control other spheres. This allows the family to function as a productive entity in which the dad works and keeps the family garden to help it grow and prosper, in safety.

Let's look at the jurisdictions for which each government is responsible. In the family government, there is responsibility to procreate and then train the generations to be productive servant-leaders in the other spheres, to engage in the private ownership of property, to aid in family training and capitalistic enterprise, and to provide for their descendants with a proper inheritance. In the church government, there is responsibility to equip believers for their respective callings by teaching sound doctrine and providing a safe community for accountability and growth; to function prophetically in society as God's representative voice to influence the other public spheres, including the civil and marketplace governments, in moral and socioeconomic matters; to engage in the ethics of conflict resolution, as arbiters, between church members; and to be the messenger of God's saving grace to lost souls. In the civil government, there is responsibility to protect law-abiding citizens by punishing those who violate just law; to establish said law based upon biblical principles; to provide for national security by raising a military force to protect the borders; and to provide a safe environment for the practice of free market enterprises. In the commercial government or marketplace, there is responsibility to trade skills and services that further promote economic growth and creative business opportunity and to exercise free market business principles that produce profit opportunities for workers engaged in those industries. As you can see this is a bird's-eye view of God's governments at work in a society, and methods change over time, thanks to technological advancements, global communication abilities, media availability, etc. However, the core responsibilities are summarized here.

Now, concerning the family gatekeeper, this societal model puts great responsibility on the man, and therefore pressure. This is intended by God to forge godly character and strength. In the face of such a challenge, it is much easier for men to let the "experts" and "officials" always cited in news reports to carry more of the weight of decision-making and dispersing of wisdom. After all, what the heck do we know about mental health, healthy sexuality, calculus or engineering, or law? We need the experts!

Ah, there is certainly a place and time for tutors, teachers, and trainers to educate in subject matters where we lack. Don't ever ask me to teach my children or grandchildren music or chemistry. This is not the issue. Rather, it is about who holds ultimate responsibility and decision-making authority for the souls, values, worldviews, and thinking processes of the children in the home. Well, the Scriptures teach us it *is* dad, but society teaches anyone *but dad* is equipped. A welfare state needs neutered dads, who cannot govern in the gate, so the state can control that gate. A healthy society is one in which each government is actively working to produce according to its purpose, and this begins with the family, which feeds the three public spheres. If God designed it this way, then He put into the man at Creation what he needs to work and protect his household as he stands in the gate.

In Bible times, the gate of a village or city was the place in which business and legal affairs were conducted, where the gatekeepers of the various spheres would meet to address issues, make covenants, and work through transactions. We recall in the book of Ruth, that Boaz, a landowner and businessman, met the other potential "redeemer" of Naomi's property, as she was a widow and unable to make ends meet. In the presence of the elders in the gate, Boaz and the other relative conducted their transaction, based upon the rules of the covenant in Israel, whereby one of them had responsibility for the widow's care to ensure generational continuity. The other relative passed and thereby transferred the right of redemption to Boaz. Notice now what is transacted between Boaz and the elders:

> Then Boaz said to the elders and all the people, "You are witnesses this day that I have bought from the hand of Naomi all that belonged to Elimelech, and all that belonged to Chilion and Mahlon. Also Ruth the Moabite, the widow of Mahlon, I have bought to be my wife, to perpetuate the name of the dead in his inheritance, that the name of the dead may not be cut off from among his brothers and from the gate of this native place. You are witnesses this day."
>
> Then all the people who were at the gate and the elders said, "We are witnesses. May the Lord make the woman, who is coming into your house, like Rachel and Leah." (Ruth 4:9–11)

What do we learn here? The "gate" is a place of redemption, protection, and government. Elders (overseers) function in the gate of their jurisdiction—this could be the family, the church, the state, or the marketplace. Gatekeepers are responsible to honor the covenant in their sphere, so the gatekeeper both "works" and "keeps" his garden. Likewise, Boaz submitted to authority, "kept his garden," and was thus empowered to govern. Furthermore, anyone seeking to transact with the family goes through the gate, which connects the walls of protection and gives safe access. Meanwhile, anyone who goes over the wall (we'll get to this) is a thief because he has bypassed the gatekeeper—dad—and is thus violating the covenant.

Second—Understand the Walls Men Are Called to Build

I have conducted more funerals and memorial services than I can count. The most read passage chosen by grieving family members is Psalm 23:1–2: "The Lord is my Shepherd. I shall not want. He makes me lie down in green pastures; He leads me beside still waters."

Notice the metaphor God uses in displaying His care, protection, and comfort to all who trust in Him—a shepherd. In ancient times, a shepherd provided everything his sheep needed for sustenance and health. We are often referred to as sheep in Scripture, which speaks of our total dependence upon Jesus. In fact, without a shepherd, a flock of sheep would not make it, then or now.

Every Scripture is given for our instruction, correction, and guidance. Thus, if we see Psalm 23 though, the lens of the principle of representation we covered in chapter 4, who then is the Divine Shepherd's human representative in the family to find green pastures and still waters for the family? The answer is the gatekeeper who stands in the gate of his family's "pasture," making it a safe place for all family members to prosper. That, my friend, is you and me, the father.

This should prompt us to seek to understand shepherds in Bible times, both their work and their approach. Let's consider a couple examples that shed light for us. We'll look at the "Christmas shepherds," and then we'll look at David, the shepherd boy.

In our home church, we of course put on a Christmas children's pageant every year, and all five of my boys at one time or another were shepherds. They wanted to be soldiers, or sword-bearing angels, so they could carry swords, but I had to explain that there were probably not many weapons at the manger scene. They put on the costumes, acted amazed, and frightened by the angels and with their friends made us all feel warm inside and happy.

Now, did you ever wonder what those shepherds did with their sheep when they ran to see the Christ Child? Did they tell them, "Hey, guys, we'll be back soon, so stay put and don't wander because there are lions and bears and coyotes out there," and the sheep gave them a thumbs-up and obeyed? Consider how Luke describes the situation: "And in the same region there were shepherds out in the field, keeping watch over their flock by night" (Luke 2:8). The word *field* in the Greek is "agros," and it means "a field, as a drive for cattle; generally the country; country, farm, piece of ground" (*Strong's Dictionary*) and "country, rather than city" (New Englishman's Greek Lexicon). The English words used in the New Testament for "agros" are "field(s); country; lands; farm." It is thus reasonable to conclude that our Christmas shepherds were as likely to be in open fields, out of town and away from farms, as they were to be on someone's farm.

The point is that sheep need an enclosure at night, a sheepfold, in which to sleep safely. Unless shepherds were near a landowner's property, caring for his sheep, in which case there might be a more permanent corral, they had to make do with what they had to protect the flock. In these cases, shepherds would gather thorny brush, possibly the type used for our Lord's crown of thorns, push them together, and create a makeshift corral wall. If a cave was nearby, they would utilize its exterior to function as part of their wall and thorny brush and stones for the remainder. They would move the flock into the corral through an opening, and the shepherd would lie down in the makeshift gate, with rod and staff, and thus become the "gatekeeper." In fact, even in permanent corrals on farms, with sturdy stone walls, there was an opening to function as the gate, without man-made doors. The man was the gatekeeper. So let's revisit Luke 2 again. "And an angel of the Lord appeared to them, and the glory of the Lord shone around them, and they were filled with fear" (Luke 2:9).

Now, if the shepherds were filled with fear, how do you think the sheep handled it? These are peaceful, conflict-avoiding creatures, who got rattled at strange or loud noises, and that's why the shepherds voice was so important as a constant in their existence to reassure and comfort them. Imagine what happened when an angel showed up who terrified their shepherds. Then, "suddenly there was with the angel a multitude of the heavenly host praising God..." (v 13). If one angel scared everyone, what would a battalion of them do? The sheep had to have been in a secure corral made by the shepherds, unless previously constructed as a more permanent structure, with the shepherds in the gate. If not, the Bethlehemites would have been eating a lot of mutton due to massive cardiac arrest among the poor sheep.

"When the angels went away from them into heaven, the shepherds said to one another, 'Let us go over to Bethlehem and see this thing that has happened'" (v 15). Here we note that the sheepfold was definitely outside of town, subject to more predators than would be in Bethlehem. So, when the shepherds took off for town, did the sheep guard themselves? Of course not. Someone was assigned with the unenviable task of staying in the gate to keep the sheep safe. This is, in itself, a great lesson for men. Being inconvenienced is actually part of our call as gatekeepers and a privilege. This is why I never believe a man that tells me he's too busy to read Scripture to his family, put his children to bed, pray with his wife, etc. What a great picture and lesson for us as we are called to keep our family gates.

Remember Genesis chapter 3 and the serpent, Eve, and Adam. The man was not in the gate, and disaster occurred. We are as responsible as Adam was to protect, comfort, and guide the family.

Now let's look at David, the "Shepherd boy." The book of 1 Samuel provides two accounts that show David's role and activities as a shepherd for his father. Jesse owned at least one flock of sheep and perhaps more; we don't know if the land on which his sheep grazed was his, or common free-range land used by all the shepherds. This lack of real estate would be why the shepherds were always moving their flocks to "green pastures" for good feeding, and calm, fresh ("still") waters for drinking. In such an area, they would construct their overnight sheepfold. David did something like this—he would have used any permanent corral structures and temporary constructions when and where necessary. So, in 1 Samuel 16, Samuel the prophet visits Jesse's town of Bethlehem to select the next king of Israel, per God's command. After considering Jesse's first seven sons and getting a thumbs-down from the Lord, this dialogue occurs: "Then Samuel said to Jesse, 'Are all your sons here?' And he said, 'There remains yet the youngest, but behold, he is keeping the sheep. And Samuel said to Jesse, 'Send and get him'" (1 Sam. 16:11). Here is the word *keep* again, this time from a different Hebrew word, meaning "to tend (a flock); i.e. pasture it; gen. to rule; by extension to associate with; pastor." Notice the similarities with "keep" in the garden of Eden which means tending to the needs, part of which requires a safe environment; while pasturing means gathering the flock in a protected area when they could peacefully eat good food. Ruling requires governmental leadership and guiding, protecting, and knowing good from bad…this includes identifying threats.

We concluded in chapter five that we are restored to Adam's responsibilities through the finished work of the second Adam, the Lord Jesus Christ. Connecting the dots again points men to the covenant seat of gatekeeper, the "family shepherd" who is commissioned to guard, guide, comfort, and provide for our families. Again, if a couple decides the wife pursues a vocation outside the home, it's their decision before God—I'm not attacking that. We cannot escape our destiny—if Luke Skywalker could not run from his destiny, how can we abandon ours? Thus, I reiterate:

> Here is the point for you and me: the second Adam, the Lord Jesus Christ, restored us through His salvific work, in our minds and souls. Thus, we can fulfill what Adam did not, by faithfully reflecting the image of our Creator through our work (by God's grace working in us), that image restored by the finished work of Christ on the cross. So, if Adam was made to be the Gatekeeper, so are we today. Wow. (Chapter 5)

Let's go back to David. Once anointed by Samuel as Israel's next king, David does what a covenant man would do. He continued to serve his father by keeping the sheep in the fields. Eventually Jesse sent him with provisions to his three brothers who were serving in the army, who were lined up against the Philistine forces. Every day, the Philistine champion Goliath came forth and basically challenged the entire nation. What did the Hebrew soldiers do? They did what Adam did when the serpent presented himself—nothing, but this time they cowered in fear. So along comes young David. He hears Goliath and is incensed: "And David said to the men who stood by him, "What shall be done for the man who kills this Philistine, and takes away the reproach from Israel? For who is this uncircumcised Philistine, that he should defy the armies of the living God?" (1 Sam. 17:26).

Are you kidding me! Does this make sense from a teenager who's spent his whole life at home working for dad? Actually, yes, for when brought before King Saul, he explains his worldview on this crisis and paints an incredible picture of the life of the Gatekeeper:

> And Saul said to David, "You are not able to go against this Philistine to fight with him, for you are but a youth, and he has been a man of war from his youth." But David said to Saul, "Your servant used to keep sheep for his father. And when there came a lion, or a bear, and took a lamb from the flock, I went after him and struck him and delivered it out of his mouth. And if it arose against me, I caught him by the beard and struck and killed him. Your servant has struck down both lions and bears, and this uncircumcised Philistine shall be like one of them, for he has defied the armies of the living God." (1 Sam. 17:33–36)

David had grown in his skills with a sling, a bow, and a spear, while tending the flocks, and used the weapons when predators attacked. We see him both caring for his flock and protecting it. He was "keeping" it, just as the Lord commissioned Adam to do to his flock, and just like we are to do to our flocks! Gents, can we see the lesson inside the lesson? When we start a family with our wives, we must learn to use the tools and weapons God gives us, and also to discern any threats to our wives and children. The Holy Scriptures are *the* tools in our hands…and yet men don't have time? What! How will we ever know a predator from a friend? How will I know which "experts" out there want to rewash my child's mind and conform it into their image? How will I prepare my children for what's beyond the walls of my sheepfold? David was a gatekeeper from a young age, which required him to work, learn, love, and be vigilant. He did not rely on the Bethlehem school system to feed and protect and prepare his sheep. Jesse taught him well. This should be every one of us!

Okay. Now that we've established who and what we are, what are the walls we are supposed to construct to provide safety and provision for our families? Remember, the shepherd lies in the gate and has to trust those walls to do their job. He cannot be everywhere at once. The Lord has provided the materials we need to construct safe sheepfolds for our families, and it revolves around what launched this book in chapter 1: our worldviews. If you agree with what you've been reading, then you have a worldview that compels the man to know what goes into building those walls around the family. In fact, once the walls are established, the man does not have to watch every move family members make. They are free to pursue whatever God has for them within the pasture provided by the constructed sheepfold. This is freeing to a dad, and to his children, because they are free to fail in a safe environment even if the failure is sin, and learn from the failure while dad has his or her back, and lets him or her grow at his or her own pace.

A man who doesn't ascribe to the covenantal worldview of gatekeeping is left by default to rely more upon experience, and other leaders, to forge and prepare his children for adult life. The standards and expectations get cloudy because he himself is not sure which principles apply, and which don't. Metaphorically speaking, his walls have huge gaps in them, and the bad guys can sneak in and harm the family. Conversely, the gaps encourage children to walk into the proverbial lions' den, like the public school cliques, without dad being aware, and get devoured by the God-hating system of autonomy to which Adam fell.

Below is essentially what comprises a man constructing safe walls for his family. First, he has a conviction of becoming a gatekeeper, with sound biblical beliefs. This first requires a conviction that the Holy Scriptures are God's final authority on Earth. Second, he has a grasp on and embraces the five points of covenant and commits to practically applying them in the home. Third, he has a clear theology from Scripture on all major doctrines. Fourth, he has a clear worldview he can explain to his children on truths like creation, salvation, purpose, representation, and objective thinking. Fifth, he has a clear philosophy of biblical child-raising from infancy to adulthood. This includes obtaining full agreement by both parents, with a commitment to applying that child-training with consistency, and establishing the hierarchy of authority when children are young. Sixth, he has a clear commitment to membership and involvement in a local church. Seventh, he has a clear set of house rules that reflect dad and mom's core values and a clear set of sanctions for breaking the rules. He also has a clear explanation of why those beliefs and rules apply, and what is expected from each family member. Eighth, he has a clear set of convictions about moral, financial, social, geo-political, and relationship issues, which is key to training the family members to spot humanism in all situations. Ninth, he has a simple, applicable plan to engage the family in the Scriptures in a fun way. We acted out more Bible stories than I can count, and I still keep wooden swords in my office. My girls loved it as well. My daughters all have back-bones. Tenth, he has a home gym of some type. We have a pull-up bar in the family room for all to use and a no-frills Spartan-type gym in the basement. Eleventh, he enjoys a regular family meal, where life's issues are discussed and debated, and provides a clear explanation of these issues to the children, with age appropriateness.

Now, this may seem unattainable, but it's actually pretty straightforward if you have the right resources. I'll recommend some to help you along. The bottom line is this: if my wife and I brought children into the world, it is on me to build a family environment that will last for generations that my heirs will pass on. This is how you do it.

PART 2

Let's Man Up to the Doctrines, Principles, and Threats That Determine My Success as the Gatekeeper

The following is an exposition of key beliefs, convictions, and practices a gatekeeper needs to embrace, as well as those challenges an emasculated culture seeks to make us embrace in its goal to neutralize men. These core principles include depravity, the unreconciled conscience, the awareness meter, passivity, adolescence and coddling, repentance, and thinking like a gatekeeper. I have learned these over forty plus years of marriage, most of which have been spent preparing our eight children, plus any dads who would listen, to face life and pursue their destinies in Christ with humility and full alertness. We are still "in process," but the Lord has given us favor in this approach.

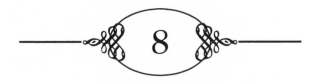

Depravity

Below is a rollout of Scriptures that address the condition of the human soul, each one followed by paraphrased headlines of *actual events* in the recent past. Proper names are omitted, as well as identifiable wording.

"The Lord saw that the wickedness of man was great in the Earth, and that every intention of the thoughts of his heart was only evil continually. And the Lord was sorry that he had made man on the Earth" (Gen. 6:5–6).

CHILD'S DEAD BODY FOUND IN
PIECES IN A 55-GALLON DRUM
JOURNALIST BRUTALLY BEATEN,
RAPED, AND MURDERED
MAN RUN OVER WITH LAWN MOWER WHILE
TRYING TO KILL HIS SON WITH CHAINSAW.
SON-IN-LAW DROVE THE MOWER

The fool says in his heart, "There is no God." They are corrupt, doing abominable iniquity; there is none who does good. God looks down from heaven on the children of man to see if there are any who understand, who seek after God. They have all fallen away; together they have become corrupt; there is none who does good, not even one. (Ps. 53:1–3).

HUSBAND MURDERS WIFE IN FRONT
OF CHILDREN, THEN KILLS THEM
BEFORE TAKING HIS OWN LIFE
MEMBER OF CONGRESS CONVICTED OF
FRAUD, EMBEZZLEMENT, AND BLACKMAIL[1]
SEVERAL COMPANIES INVOLVED
IN CONSTRUCTION FRAUD

There is a generation who curse their fathers and do not bless their mothers. There are those who are clean in their own eyes but are not washed of their filth. There are those—how lofty are their eyes, how high their eyelids lift! There are those whose teeth are swords, whose fangs are knives, to devour the poor from the face of the Earth. (Prov. 30:11–14)

CHILD SEXUAL ABUSE IS RAMPANT
IN THE MUSLIM NATION OF—
EIGHT-YEAR-OLD CHILD RAPED
WHILE VILLAGE DOES NOTHING
COMMUNIST LEADER MURDERS MILLIONS
OF HIS OWN COUNTRYMEN

"The heart is deceitful above all things, and desperately sick; who can understand it?" (Jer. 17:9).

MAN ARRESTED FOR CONSTRUCTING LARGE
BOMB

---

[1] Note: Having grown up in New York State, I've lost count of the politicians at the state level convicted of various corruptions.

IN THE NATION OF——, SIMPLY REFERRING TO A PERSON AS A MALE, IF THEY GENDER IDENTIFY THEMSELVES TO BE A FEMALE, COULD BE CONSIDERED OFFENSIVE BY THE LATTER, WHO CAN THEN REPORT IT TO LOCAL POLICE AS A "HATE INCIDENT." THE ACCUSED COULD BE POTENTIALLY PROSECUTED FOR A HATE CRIME[2]

SUSPECT TARGETED FAMILY MEMBERS IN SHOOTING SPREE

"Therefore God gave them up in the lusts of their hearts to impurity, to the dishonoring of their bodies among themselves, because they exchanged the truth about God for a lie and worshiped and served the creature rather than the Creator" (Rom. 1:24–25).

SEX TRAFFICKING OF CHILDREN BECOMING AN EPIDEMIC IN THE NATIONS OF——,——,——

PRISON GUARDS CONVICTED OF ONGOING RAPES OF FEMALE INMATES

MAN CONVICTED OF RITUAL KILLING IN WHICH MAJORITY OF VICTIMS' ORGANS HAD BEEN REMOVED

None is righteous, no, not one; no one understands; no one seeks for God. All have turned aside; together they have become worthless; no one does good, not even one. Their throat is an open grave; they use their tongues to deceive. The venom of wasps is under their lips. Their mouth is full of curses and bitterness. Their feet are swift to shed blood; in their paths are ruin and misery, and the way of peace they

---

[2] Wow.

111

have not known. There is no fear of God before their eyes. (Rom. 3:11–18)

TERRORIST GROUP BEHEADS THEIR PRIS-
ONERS AND VIDEOS IT FOR WORLD TO SEE. THEY
THREATEN ALL CHRISTIANS WITH THE SAME FATE

PARENTS SENTENCED TO LIFE IN PRISON FOR
THE ABUSE AND MURDER OF THEIR THREE-YEAR-
OLD CHILD

TWO HIGH SCHOOL STUDENTS FOUND
HANGED IN THEIR SCHOOL WERE FIRST STRAN-
GLED TO DEATH AND THEN HANGED WHILE
ALREADY DEAD

MOST CHRISTIAN DENOMINATIONS IN
NATION OF——BEING TARGETED FOR ELIMINATION
BY RADICAL, VIOLENT RELIGIOUS SECT

And you were dead in the trespasses and sins in which you once walked, following the course of this world, following the prince of the power of the air, the spirit that is now at work in the sons of disobedience—among whom we all once lived in the passions of our flesh, carrying out the desires of the body and the mind, and were by nature children of wrath. (Eph. 2:1–3)

HIGH SCHOOL TEACHER ARRESTED
FOR SEX WITH YOUNG STUDENT[3]
EMPEROR LIGHTS CHRISTIANS ON FIRE
TO ILLUMINATE HIS GARDENS

---

[3] This has happened so often across America in the last few years that I put in words above a typical situation—there have been countless teachers and students in sexual encounters, and usually the teacher is a female who is a wife and mother. How incredibly sad.

WOMAN BRAIN-DEAD AFTER BEING
SHOT IN NECK WHILE DRIVING
DICTATOR COMMITS GENOCIDE
AGAINST HIS OWN PEOPLE
THE CITY OF——SEES RECORD HIGHS IN
MURDERS AND VIOLENT CRIME
TV/MOVIE CELEBRITY CHARGED WITH
SEXUAL ASSAULT AND RAPE
RECORD NUMBER OF STDS OCCURING IN AMERICA
PLEDGE OF ALLEGIANCE, IN GOD
WE TRUST, BOTH EVICTED

I could go on and on with more horrific examples that confirm what the Holy Scriptures tell us about the human soul—it is depraved, meaning it has a natural inclination to sin and not to seek God. The apostle Paul drives this home with his blistering exposé of every one of us, without exception, in Ephesians 2:1–3. He makes it clear that we are sinful according to our nature, following the ways of the evil father—the devil—when he describes us as "sons of disobedience," which speak of our spiritual family DNA. It is a sin-filled spiritual gene that we all inherited from Adam. The result is there is no sin too barbaric nor evil for human beings to commit. We are capable of the worst from birth, having inherited original sin from Adam.

This is probably the most important doctrine for a gatekeeper to comprehend and embrace, as it explains the root cause of all wickedness, crime, and evil in a society. Everything boils down to the corrupt nature of the human soul. It helps us understand our own children and how to teach them what is happening around them and why.

I like to encourage people—hopefully, I speak courage into their souls. Many times over the years I have said to a brother, "You're a good man." I trust this blesses them, and yet, I risk speaking a nontruth into them, for even Jesus told the people not to call Him good, as He said only the Father was. He was speaking of inherent moral goodness, which is at the core of all humanist belief systems—that we are basically good people trying to do good in a difficult world, in bad environments, and dysfunctional experiences. The Bible tells us this is not true at all. The human soul's natural inclination is to sin.

Ironically these problematic societal causes are not causes at all—they are just fruit on the tree of depravity. For it is depravity that causes dysfunction and corrupt environments. It's always the root of problems, from the garden until now, and it will never change. I realize psychology professors produce textbooks for their students as society chases after answers in its quest to explain and resolve society's ills. The problem is they assume the human soul is inherently good. It is not...neither yours nor mine. Their motive is noble. The premise is not.

This is where the rubber meets the road because parents cannot bear the thought of their children being evil by nature. Of course, just go shopping with them for a day and you'll be convinced otherwise. The refusal of young parents today, across this land, to embrace honest doctrine about the soul, has launched a hybrid Christian humanism in child-raising that is such a failure that parents are looking anywhere they can to find answers and help. The answers are in the Scriptures cited above, which will change dad's life if he has the courage to read them objectively, without his own humanistic opinion, and embrace what they teach.

It's actually freeing to learn the truth, because when my young children start acting like little devils, I understand why. I don't need to panic and can get my guidance from Scripture as to how to deal with it. Of course I've heard parents explain away those passages as for another time, like under that Old Testament God, or that they're simply not as relevant today with the amazing progress of psychology and its cutting-edge modern methods that are more tender and compassionate.

Ya know what? I can't think of many things more compassionate than delivering my child from the self-destructive tendencies of his or her own depravity, the way the Lord intended for it to happen. A gatekeeper leaves his conflicted emotions outside the room when he must deal with sin in his family. He cannot bring godly government without an objective view of sin, the soul, and his family. I know, because I had to fight off those humanist sentiments for eight different children and for the spiritual sons and daughters Sandra and I have brought into the family over the years.

Why do bad things happen? People are corrupt inside. Why do children act like demons at times? They are corrupt inside. It is their nature to do so until the Holy Spirit would mercifully give them a new nature in Christ. Even then, the flesh never stops lusting, and we need the Lord's grace daily to overcome it. Why do men bail on their families by leaving the Gate unguarded? It's difficult, and painful at times, to have to confront the depraved souls of our children. Yet, if we don't do it, who will? You guessed it—nobody. Their depravity goes unchecked, and by the time they turn eighteen, dad and mom are ready to buy them off with an overpriced college experience, just to let them "go experience the world as adults, finally." The problem is that in their souls, they are not adults, because the gatekeeper never shepherded them through the war of governing their own souls, to rein in the passions of their depravity. What a mess. They get to college and…you don't want to know.

Look, I'm not saying for a moment that my family is perfect or ideal, beginning with me. Even now at my advancing age, I get the hankerings to let some jerk "have it" in the jaw just because he's a jerk. So I am still battling the flesh; we all are. And our children are far from perfect, and a few have given us a run for our money and caused us pain. No one has more power over the hearts of parents than their children. That said, we embraced the Bible's teaching on this, and as a result, we brought godly government into the home so that in the midst of fights, tempers, unkindnesses, etc., we had a peaceful home and still do. Conflicts were not allowed to go unresolved, and acts of depravity were dealt with biblically for all eight children. I was an equal opportunity punisher and restorer. By God's grace, I refused to worship at the altar of Christian humanism (i.e., the belief we are inherently good).

The Bible works! The Lord pours out His favor upon men willing to stand in the gate for their families and do it His way.

The Unreconciled Conscience

I brought more than my share of baggage into our marriage—enough for both of us—so I needed to learn how to deal with shame and walk with a clear conscience before God. Then I had to lead my children into that pasture, so their souls could find rest beside still waters.

I didn't go to counseling—I went to the cross of Christ and began a journey of dying to my own rights, ambitions, and wants. Some counsel was part of the journey, mainly from my spiritual father, Vernice Smith, who taught me the power of humility and repentance before the throne of a just and holy God. Most of the work was done repenting in God's presence and learning how to receive not only forgiveness but also the cleansing of my conscience.

We addressed this in chapter 6 with "Adam's fatal response," in which we learned that he ran from the Sin Remover and hid in his shame. A man then makes fig leaves to cover himself and turns to overemotional, abusive, deceiving, controlling, abdicating, or other tormented behaviors, to shift attention to others in hopes of not being found out. Now this is the bondage of an unreconciled conscience, which is at war with its Creator, in a state of constant hiding and will never find peace unless confession and repentance happen.

"If we confess our sins, He is faithful to forgive us our sins and to cleanse us from all unrighteousness" (1 John 1:9). When a man truly believes this, his life will be revolutionized, because he will realize that the Lord Jesus already suffered and atoned for our every sin, no matter how vile, so that God is waiting to offer instant forgiveness. But it does not stop there. *All* unrighteousness from that sin is removed and we are cleansed so that our mind and spirit are restored to perfect harmony with the Father and no record of that sin exists on our souls! This is because the Lord has imputed, or legally transferred, the righteousness of Jesus to us, so forgiveness and restoration to our relationship as sons is instant.

It doesn't get any better than this. So thanks to Vernice Smith, I began to practice this early on in our marriage. Eventually it began to take root in my soul, as I read the Scriptures regularly (hint) and saw the guarantee of this amazing act of mercy in Old Testament and New. My state of mental health continually improved, the torment ended, and I bask daily in His endless mercies, without apology, because Jesus gave everything for me to enjoy it. I dare not insult the Lord's sacrifice with self-righteous fig-leafing and excuse-making. He wants no excuse, because there are none. He wants repentance—end of ball game—because He did all the work, and He gets all the glory. This will lift a lifetime's worth of weight off the man who embraces the truth and enjoys what Jesus already did.

Now, move on to the children. It's challenging enough for an adult man to grasp this, but a child's conscience simply is not there yet. So the gatekeeper is to shepherd his children to the still waters of forgiveness and cleansing. The more we cater to their depraved behavior, the more guilt piles up in their little souls and the more they act out their torment. They aren't in charge so their fig-leafing finds release in various forms of running and hiding from the guilt in temper tantrums, blatant disobedience, subtle and sneaky disobedience, moodiness, disrespect, fighting, bullying, mocking, lying, withdrawing, etc. Get the picture? The child's conscience is at war with his mind and soul, and all he knows is that he must somehow hide, just like Adam did! This is the natural behavior of a depraved soul—he can't help it. That is where dad comes to the rescue, rather literally. When proper government is applied, punishment is administered to fit the crime (sin), but it doesn't end there. Ending there is the humanist way, which lets the child boil in an unresolved state. Rather, our children need to be led to and through 1 John 1:9.

Why do we get to enjoy divine mercy but deprive our children of it? It's not complicated. This is what Sandra and I do. First, we clearly explain the sin and ensure the child understands it and that the sin is against God and whomever (usually some family member). Second, we review with the child the Scriptures. I had them all memorize the Living Bible translation of Proverbs 20:30 which says, "Punishment that hurts chases evil from the heart." Consider the Amplified Version: "Blows that wound cleanse away evil, and strokes reach to the innermost parts." This third step is critical as it is the ideal opportunity to teach them the covenant model in family life.

- We submit to the One True God   (Transcendence)
- He delegated His authority to Dad and Mom   (Representation)
- We have family rules, based upon the Bible   (Ethics)
- Punishment is earned for breaking the rules   (Sanctions)
- After the punishment, full restoration is granted   (Renewal)

In explaining this probably hundreds of times over the years, proper punishment is administered, under control, in a predictable manner. The punishment doesn't change—the child knows what to expect, always. Once the tears stop, we ask the child why he was punished and have him explain. Fourth, then we explain, it is my love for the child that caused us to punish him—because we don't want "evil in his heart" (the unresolved guilt and resulting shame). We explain that now as he asks God's forgiveness, and yours, that all sin is forgiven and cleansed, removed, and washed away. Fifth, we have the child pray, asking God's forgiveness, then ours. If a family member has been wronged, he goes to that member and asks forgiveness. Lastly, once the child asks for forgiveness, we say *yes*, hug, tickle, wrestle, crack jokes…make the child laugh!

Why this last step? So the child can experience the reality of divine cleansing—that God's delegated representatives to him, Dad and Mom, do *not* hold the sin against him at all, just as God Himself has forgiven and cleansed, thus restoring him to a perfectly right relationship with all parties.

This is the covenant in action. This is redemption in action. The gatekeeper's primary motive along the path of life should always be redemptive—restoring that child, adult, spiritual son or daughter, to right relationship with the Lord God, and his or her fellow humans. This removes fig leaves and allows him or her to walk into a room and have healthy fellowship with his or her family, friends, church community, etc., without guilt and being fully accepted. When the gatekeeper practices this with his children, they will learn to live it out at young ages and walk in health in their souls. This is not to say they won't choose to sin as adults—we all do—but they have embedded in their souls the miracle of covenant renewal.

If this all sounds rather straightforward and simple, it's because it is. Do we honestly think the Lord would complicate fathering in such a way that we have to find an "expert" to get the answers? No, it's in black and white in His revealed will—the Holy Scriptures.

Now I didn't say it was easy. It's not complicated, but the heart-strings of humanism, laziness, or our own unresolved guilt will gang up on us to talk us out of getting the job done. Sometimes, a well-meaning family member or friend will do the honors and thereby serve up a heaping plate of guilt as he or she tells us there must be a better way—perhaps we should get some counseling, eh? Notice the subtlety—counseling has a role in life but not in a way that nullifies the living power of the Holy Scriptures. I choose God's way.

I refused to listen to those lies and instead sucked it up, remembered to think objectively about what I was doing and why, and then got the job done. As a result, dinnertime was fun, provoking and entertaining in our home, with no unresolved conflicts on anyone's plates. You owe it to your children to get them through 1 John 1:9.

Our third son, Zach, the fourth born in the family, was a piece of work as a child. If there was an award for getting into trouble in the family, Zach would have set records. He had thin skin and a short fuse (a bit like his dad when I was young) and had no problem picking fights with his two older brothers. This was always a bad move on his part as evidenced by how the fights ended, but Zach would not back down.

So the challenge for me was to guide his conscience into wholeness with God and the family through discipline and healthy reconciliation first with God, then his siblings, then himself. I kept a small desk in my office at church; so when Sandra would call and tell me, "Come home and get him. He's at it again," I'd run home, grab Zach, and he'd finish his school work that day at the office with me, while things cooled down.

Amid this battle, the Lord showed me a fiercely loyal and tenacious son, who wanted to know his place in not just the family, but in life; and who wanted to be like his dad. What a great heart he showed. Not to mention he was hilarious and a delight when he was on. My job was to keep him "on."

So we spent more time in the "reconciliation room" than I did with the others since Zach needed it more. At times he wanted no part of it and wanted to give me a hard time. Then something amazing would happen. Amid his punishment, I'd ask him the relevant questions and then encouraged him to open up to me. So he did, and I learned about the loyal, thoughtful soul my son had, and how he wanted the best for his brothers but felt lesser at times and needed to prove himself. So he fought. That's what I did as a boy, and we talked about it, and he began to trust me.

After the punishment was applied, he'd offer heartfelt prayers of repentance to the Lord that I knew were real. His brothers weren't so sure about that at the time, and now I understand why, but as a gatekeeper the Lord wanted me to see it so I could see the man he would become. There was no way I was leaving his conscience unreconciled to let guilt and condemnation live in his mind. I showed Zach more patience than the others.

As he got older he still battled in his conscience, and it got him into some problems. The beauty of it was that he came right to me to both tell me and ask for help. We walked together through it, and Sandra and I watched him grow into noble manhood through a tough season. The key was Zach keeping his heart open and honest with the Lord, practicing repentance, and letting his conscience heal.

I am incredibly proud of my boy, and when I'm out of town, he calls me regularly to stand with me on my journey. Another great gift he gave me was his love and loyalty to my mom. He touched her heart in ways no one else could or did. She's passed on now, but I watched her and Zach walk in a loving, fruitful relationship. Zach brought honor to all of us in the family.

In the end, the tough journey to a reconciled conscience was more than worth it.

The Awareness Meter

Many years ago, I was asked to give the message at my friend's memorial service. He was a great man who was loving, kind, patient, and humble. I was honored that the family selected me. The church was packed, with folks having arrived from all over the country to honor our brother. After the service, I was greeting many old friends, and one man approached me, gave his greeting, and then began to tell me all about his ministry experiences in different cities. I listened out of courtesy for a bit and then excused myself. Of course, what I really wanted to say was, "What is wrong with you? We are burying our brother and honoring him, and all you can talk about is yourself? I don't care at all about your ministry nor how great thou art." However, knowing that Sandra would let me have it for such indiscretion, I bit my tongue until I could make an exit. Why am I telling you this story? It's because of a major male crisis today: the broken *awareness meter* in men.

Consider Solomon's counsel on this matter:

> Know well the condition of your flocks, and give attention to your herds, for riches do not last forever; does a crown endure to all generations? When the grass is gone and the new growth appears and the vegetation of the mountains is gathered, the lambs will provide your clothing, and the goats the price of a field. There will be

enough goats' milk for your food, for the food of
your household and maintenance for your girls.
(Prov. 27:23–27)

As we grasp again the metaphor of God as our Shepherd and
the gatekeeper as God's representative for the family, the lesson is
clear—always be aware of every situation, at home, work and play;
the health of the souls and spiritual conditions of you, your wife, and
children; the influences in their lives (Is someone or thing trying to
come over the wall?); the needs you foresee in each of them including
the strengths in each you need to nurture, the weaknesses you need
to cover, and the training and guidance you need to provide to take
them to the next level.

The inherent call of all gatekeepers is to be influencers and inves-
tors in others. Other living beings in the room have legitimate needs:
the need for you to listen more and talk less. Sandra and I are amazed
at how often we'll run into someone after months or years of not seeing them and not one question will be asked of us, like, "So are you
all still alive?", "What is God doing in your lives these days?", or "Still
have eight children, or have they all flown the coup?" You know, the
basic courtesies that actually don't exist anymore. Rather, they talk
about themselves, and then themselves, and when finished with that,
tell us about themselves. They literally don't ask one question.

Now let me ask you a question. With so many people in our
culture running around with unresolved guilt and a closet full of
fig leaves for every issue, how refreshing, inviting, and encouraging
would it be for them to run into you, who shows great interest in
their souls, lives, family, work, hobbies, etc.? Think about it. If hardly
anyone has an awareness meter that works, who is going to actually
invest in these folks? The answer is those gatekeepers who put others
first, like my friend did, like Jesus does. After all, if His Spirit dwells
within us, shouldn't we move "self" out of the way and let Him do
His thing? According to Jesus, this is normal. "All authority in heaven
and on Earth has been given to me. Go therefore and make disciples
of all nations" (Matt. 28:18–19). Would God delegate such authority
and mission to us without giving us the awareness meter to see and

hear what is going on, and respond with His ministry to people? It's time to repent for self-centered awareness-killing and wake up to the world around us, beginning with our families.

I grilled into my children from when they were young to intentionally ask questions of others, regardless of that person's lack of interest in them. I explained that they are the covenant influencers, not influencees, and this simple discipline puts them ahead of the game every time.

My fourth son, Trevor, is both kind-hearted and strong as a bull. He's easygoing and friendly and, like my son-in-law, Ben, loves to have a good time. I always saw a shepherding heart in him (not necessarily in church ministry but in life) and encouraged him to think of others first by practicing awareness.

It wasn't tough to do because even when he was young, he was usually happy and infected others with his smile and love for life. Still, our flesh is self-centered so he had to practice awareness to make it an effective habit.

Then along came Julianna, who captured Trev's heart and ours. Jules is the daughter of my good friend Dave Meyer, probably the kindest person I know. Jules has her dad's kindness in her. Whenever I get back to New York, Trev and Jules always take the time to ask me about my life, my health, the work I'm doing in ministry, and so on. It blesses me because so few people ask such questions. Jules has a great awareness meter like her dad, and Trev has grown in this area more than he realizes.

Jules owns a salon and is killing it because she cares and asks questions (and she's really good at her skill set). People love her, and people love Trev. Trev can be so in tune with me because he pays attention, that he'll question my moods, or challenge me to rise to the task at hand yet does so with encouragement. He does the same for other men who seek him out because his awareness meter makes him a safe place and a wise conduit of God's insight.

Trev and Zach are close, and Trev stood with his brother when Zach was dealing with his adversity and deposited trusted wisdom because he was a safe place. What a great gift to offer others. I practice awareness often, but I lack Trevor's inherent patience. He and Jules make me very proud as they are living out our worldview in the routine of life.

Passivity

I seldom go to a shopping mall as they don't pique my interest. I suppose if my bank account were overflowing I'd treat myself to some nice gear. What does interest me is what, or who, walk out of the mall, and what they immediately do, or are already in process of doing. Have you guessed it yet? The head is down, the walk is clueless; one hand is holding the cell phone, and the owner is owned by the phone. Most of these captives of passivity are young on the age spectrum. It's a sad but dangerous picture, especially in light of the slow death of the awareness meter in both men and women. Do you see the issue? They are receptors, the prey, the unaware. These are the fruits of passivity. No one seems aware of their surroundings, and life just happens to them, around them, and through them, and they are helpless to cut off the influence and change the story. They just receive and fall further into passivity.

Restaurants show us the disease has spread to parents as well. Just observe the waiting area for being seated. Entire families will be on a bench and all of them on their phones. They are practically oblivious to the stimuli of life around them. What if potential danger has entered the room? Who's aware of this, or who should be? The gatekeeper. I always look everywhere when I enter a store, restaurant, shop, etc., and I sit facing the door.

Seldom does anyone initiate conversation in a waiting area to engage in prolonged conversation. Perhaps one offers a comment or two, and then all heads are down again. This is what I observe in every eating establishment I might visit. It never fails to happen. The new passive American family is hard at work initiating nothing and provoking or inspiring nothing in one another. Of course the trends in a family begin in the gate, and a passive dad does not confront the influences and interested visitors that want to mess with the souls and minds of his wife and children. A gatekeeper is an initiator of defense, looking to drop the enemy for a loss, not invite him into the huddle!

Passive means to be "influenced, acted upon, or affected by some external force, cause or agency; being the object of action rather than causing action [opposed to active]; not participating readily or actively" (Dictionary.com). It took less than three chapters in the first book of the Bible for passivity to manifest itself in Adam. He was influenced by and acted upon by both the serpent and Eve. When the bad guy, or the flesh, or the subtle tricks of modern culture are the influencers, and the man is the influencee, the fruit of his passivity puts the family in danger, first spiritually, then emotionally, then intellectually, and finally even physically.

The gatekeeper represents something beyond himself to his children. What do we think children will absorb from dad if he models passivity to them? They will not know who they are, why they're on the Earth, nor how to find purpose. And worst of all, they will not know who this great and loving Savior is that calls them to a destiny. They just survive, living life as receivers of the influences around them, while their gatekeeper lets it all happen.

The irony of passivity in men is that we don't even realize it has captured us, because we assume it's "just life" happening. The thought of being proactive, of invading life, of capturing the souls of our children, of intentionally being a blessing to friends and strangers, doesn't register as part of our reality. Life happens to us. This is not how the Lord planned it. Rather,

> So God created man in His own image,
> in the image of God He created him; male and
> female He created them. And God blessed them.
> And God said to them, 'Be fruitful and multiply
> and fill the Earth and subdue it and have domin-

ion over the fish of the sea and over the birds
of the heavens and over every living thing that
moves upon the Earth. (Gen. 1:27–28)

Notice the image of the Creator put in us gives us an inherent
design to produce, to bear fruit, to lead, and to initiate.

Notice in Psalm 8, that after Adam fell and was cursed and
passed the original sin to all of us, that the inherent call to fulfill our
purpose at Creation in Genesis 1:27–28 is still intact?

"What is man that you are mindful of him, and the son of man
that you care for him? Yet you have made him a little lower than the
heavenly beings and crowned him with glory and honor. You have
given him dominion over the works of your hands; you have put all
things under his feet" (Ps. 8:4–6).

When God pronounced His curse upon Adam, He never
removed the call; rather, He declared that it would be tougher to get
it done as the ground would bear a curse. Thorns and thistles would
grow like weeds, and we'd have to sweat with hard work to accomplish the task. Such resistance did not exist before the fall.

Consider Jesus's teaching about the talents in Matthew 25:14–
30. A ruler gave his three servants five, two, and one talent, respec-
tively. A talent was a unit of money worth about twenty years'
wages—in other words, these servants were given a lot of pressure
and responsibility. He gave "to each according to his ability" in verse
15, thus giving them opportunity to capitalize upon the situation as
each had the inherent ability to make it happen as we saw in Genesis
1:27–28. The first two servants doubled their share, while the third
practiced passivity—"but he who had received the one talent went
and dug in the ground and hid his master's money" (Matt. 25:18).
When the ruler returned, he rewarded the first two with greater
opportunity and position, while he punished the passive guy and
"cast the worthless servant into the outer darkness" (v 30). The ruler
(i.e., Jesus) made a declaration about how we are to live life: "For to
everyone who has will more be given, and he will have an abundance.
But from the one who has not, even what he has will be taken away"
(Matt. 25:29). The context is, that the first two invested themselves

in what God gave them, and multiplied it, and thus are given even more, while the one who hid it and produced nothing, lost even what he had.

As harsh as this seems, it fits cleanly with man's created purpose in Genesis. The third servant is a picture of passivity, and Jesus teaches us that we bring sanctions upon ourselves, which obviously impact our families, if we are the gatekeepers. We need to put an end to passivity, friends. We actually have amazing grace, because we are made in the image of the Lord Jesus Christ, and passivity is not "spiritually normal" for believers. I recommend this: get on your knees right now, repent for passivity, and ask the Lord to kill passivity in you and put you on the path of covenant sonship.

When my oldest son, Justin, was young he had a knack for making money even then. I realized God put in him an entrepreneurial bent—a truly risky path to take. Nevertheless, I encouraged him in it and began to explain if he were to ever lead his own companies he'd need to conquer the passivity that robs our initiative.

We were able to arrange an apprenticeship for him with a team of brothers and their dad, who had built a successful construction and property management business. He did a few tough years under their thumb and at times did not like it because it challenged his unredeemed desire, at the time, to be his own boss.

There were more than a few talks between us about his embracing the cross and absorb all he could not just from their skills but their motivating passion to get it done and always do it well. We all have passive tendencies, and the Lord brings some benevolent taskmaster to take us to the crossroad of broken submission.

By God's grace, Justin hung in there and subsequently at a young age began his own company. He made his share of mistakes with people and projects (don't we all), but I noticed that the brothers' passion for getting after it and doing it till the end had been imparted to him. Meanwhile, I had been imparting the following into his soul whenever I had the opportunity: "Son, the best antidote to mediocrity and failure is humility and teachableness because our Lord delights in empowering broken vessels. You have a strong gift, and passivity wants you to take it for granted. As you walk in an intentional humility and remain teachable to the wisdom of others, God will starve that passivity, and He'll bless you." Eventually, those words took root and good things happened.

Passivity would have killed the dream because anyone self-employed has to stay motivated to be an initiator when and where others won't or can't. Justin married Amanda, who is a daughter to me, and they worked hard to build a marriage, then a business, then a family (they have five) who reflect their biblical values. Now, my son is a nobleman in Christ, and he is intentionally looking for ways to practically train his children in business and leadership. They are essentially apprenticing under him in his property and management company, which has grown into two states.

My daughter-in-law is my son's best friend, and my grandchildren are thriving under their leadership in the oneness of marriage. Killing passivity was a key for this to happen.

As we bring this section to a close, following is a list of examples of what passivity is, and what it is not, to help you on your way.

Passivity is
> Checking your cell phone regularly for "the latest"
> Reading only the comics or novels
> Binge watching (more than about twice a year)
> Saying "I'm gonna start reading the Bible"
> Looking, talking, acting like all the world around you
> Thinking whatever is culturally acceptable is normal
> Shaving only when the mood strikes
> Avoiding deep issues with your family
> Letting father time slowly bury your challenges and weaknesses
> Attending a church mainly because you like it
> Letting life happen to you

Passivity is not
> Staying under authority
> Following a budget every week

Buying wisely what you both need and like
Putting others first
Questioning the "experts" floating around
Speaking honestly and regularly with Jesus
Reading the Scriptures regularly and intelligently
Attending a church where you and your family can serve
Hating your sins
Repenting regularly
Enjoy the ride—it's well worth it.

Adolescence and Coddling

When Justin, my eldest son, was five or six years old, I got a call from Sandra informing me that Justin got into a fight with another boy who was picking on our son's friend. I then asked her only one question. Can you guess? "How did he do?" While Sandra was doing a great job in not rescuing the children from the daily pains of life, this was new ground for her, and she was a bit appalled at my response. After all, isn't fighting also a sin and a terrible example?

I explained my two conclusions to the situation to her. First, Justin stood up for his friend. I'll take that all day long. In fact, I told my boys continually when they were young to defend their sisters at all cost. My eldest took the noble path. Second, if learning the skills of self-defense were key to David while watching the sheep, they are good enough for us Tallo men. Some people have said that was the Old Testament speaking, to which I simply ask, "Are people no longer depraved and 'by nature children of wrath'?" Of course, unless that soul is regenerated in Christ, born from above, born again, he is capable of evil deeds against humanity.

Does anyone else see something rather strange about this passage, or am I just the weird one?

> Hear, O sons, a father's instruction, and be attentive, that you may gain insight, for I give you good precepts; do not forsake my teaching. When I was a son with my father, tender, the only

one in the sight of my mother, he taught me and said to me, "Let your heart hold fast my words; keep my commandments and live. Get wisdom; get insight; do not forget, and do not turn away from the words of my mouth." (Prov. 4:1–5)

This is Solomon recording his experience with his dad, King David, before his mother had any other children yet. He was very young. In fact, he refers to his very young self as "tender," which means "by implication weak; faint [hearted], soft" according to *Strong's Dictionary*. Here are some uses of this Hebrew word *rak* for tender in the Old Testament:

And Abraham ran to the herd and took a calf, *tender* and good. (Gen. 18:7; emphasis added)

But Jacob said to him [Esau], My lord knows that the children are *frail*. (Gen. 33:13; emphasis added)

Like gentle rain upon the *tender* grass. (Deut. 32:2)

Clearly this word for "tender" does not depict mature strength or seasoned wisdom and character but rather a state of neediness in the early stages of life. Yet David took Solomon aside at this "tender" age and launched into a litany of deep teaching as recorded in these many chapters of the book of Proverbs. Surely this is not your typical adolescent counsel. This is, rather, a father expecting his young son to begin grasping the principles of life sooner than later. David didn't wait until his son was what we consider to be ready, aged eighteen or later. The Israelites acknowledged a youngster developing from child-hood to young adulthood to an adult man or woman. A teenaged boy was a young man, ready for the burdens and responsibilities of young manhood such as guarding his father's sheep and killing any predators that posed a threat. It worked pretty well for David, didn't it?

Do we find it rather bizarre that we recognize physical puberty— usually in the early teens, whereby a young couple can conceive a child, and of course the experts seek to guide them toward safe sex—yet we expect no mental or emotional maturity from these same youngsters. So they can procreate, but they're incapable of responsible behavior, leadership, deep thought, and intelligent communication, skill development, and productive work? Sorry, the Scriptures don't buy this lie as they give no provision for an adolescent stage in which a young man or woman can copulate but not grow in calling under healthy family government.

This is my own definition of adolescence as exists in our culture:

> A contrived stage of life in which society recognizes the physical ability to procreate and thereby bring life into the world, while expecting no societal contributions intellectually, morally, emotionally, financially, or physically. Rather, the teen years are a time for extending childhood playtime at a teen level, and to be catered to, entertained, and sheltered from life's routine challenges and pressures.

Think about it. We are called to prepare our young sons to be gatekeepers one day, not excuse-makers; and our daughters to be strong, virtuous leaders that know who they are, and yet are not intimidated by men. The myth of adolescence robs a father of about one-half of their child's life, during which he or she could be trained and prepared for life. Thus, today's finished product is an unfinished and insecure soul that runs from pressure and responsibility, expecting dad, mom, and teacher to grease the skids for them. These are society's future leaders? No, thanks. In fact, many adolescents end up on a college campus, on dad's dime, to extend their years of play, hopefully in tandem with some study time. This is not an argument against a college education, as long as it's not a rip-off. Rather, an adolescent mindset usually doesn't evolve into fully orbed adulthood in the typical campus experience. I know, I've been there. A man or woman needs to be an adult before taking the first class.

A rational look at many heroes of the Bible reveal an amazing fact—many were in their teen years when God began to use them and challenge them. Joseph, son of Jacob, was enslaved as a teen and was soon running Potiphar's house. David, son of Jesse, killed Goliath around seventeen to eighteen years old and then became a captain in Saul's army, leading successful campaigns. Daniel was enslaved by Babylon between fifteen and about twenty-two years old and then became the fearless and prophetic advisor to the kings of Babylon. Joseph and Mary were probably both teens, as Jewish men were typically expected to be married by eighteen; hence the arranged marriages. Jesus's twelve disciples, other than Matthew, were all probably around eighteen to twenty, give or take a few years. Consider the example of John and James. The mother of John and James was a bit of a meddler, campaigning for her boys to have seats of honor near Jesus. Had they been married, she would not have gotten involved like that; hence they were at best at marrying age. In another example, Jesus instructed Peter to pay the temple tax with the coin in the mouth of the fish, which was only enough for the two of them. We learn in Exodus 30:14 that Israelite men above age twenty have to pay the tax. Jesus only provided tax money for Peter, while saying nothing to the other men, who were probably under twenty years old. After all, Jesus would not break Old Testament law by ignoring anyone else required to pay.

Consider the following logic. The education for typical Jewish men was completed at around age fifteen. If the family could afford it and he was accepted, the son then put in years of training under a rabbi. If not, he entered the workforce, often apprenticing under his father or another mentor.

I trust we get the point from these amazing examples. Sons and daughters were trained to carry progressive levels of responsibility in their early teens, with the expectation that they would be "marryable" by around eighteen (yes, I made that word up). As they married, they entered the full adult community around them and took on the adult burdens of provision and raising a family.

Consider the pressure Joseph faced when Mary gave him the great news that she was pregnant. He didn't run away, but rather, he ran *into* the problem, to find an honorable way to divorce Mary and not shame her. This is a young man who *is* a man, ready for the trials of life…in his case, raising the Christ! By the way, Joseph and Mary were sinners, just like you and me, who were sovereignly chosen by God for the task, again, just like you and me, and just like our children. So are we preparing our sons and daughters for divine destiny, or are we giving them spending money to buy weed on campus, having already paid their tuition? Not trying to be cynical, but realistic. If everything is handed to my son, why would he want to become a man?

Now, the other dangerous tendency when we buy into adolescence is rescuing our children from the regular pains of life, thinking we are sparing them something, which ironically will hit them head-on as adults. When they are young, it is the time to awaken their awareness to life's unfairness due to the depravity of the human race and a fallen creation. We already covered this problem.

Before Jesse sent David into the fields to take charge of his flocks, he prepared him to use his weapons, to protect the sheep, to confront the predators. He then let him experience the cold, the dark, the dangers of life in the fields. He did not fight his battles for him; no, he let him bleed a bit if that's what it took to kill a lion, but he did prepare him. Also, someone, probably Jesse or his wife, inspired David in his love of music and showed him how to worship. Then they left him to his solitary nights in the fields to write and compose most of the book of Psalms. They prepared the "whole person" in their youngest son.

Many times I have seen young moms launch into panic mode when her child falls on the playground or gets run into or over by someone bigger. Emotion takes charge, which causes hysteria in the child, which he or she is being trained to express! Alternatively, if after *calmly* taking an honest look to determine the extent of the injury and finding it to be minor, like the bumps of life, the mom calms her child, comforts him or her, and then sends him or her back into the life of the playground, she does him or her a huge favor. That child is thus being prepared to face life's trials with calm, courage, and faith.

In 1996 when Sandra and I bought our old farm house, the boys and I began to rebuild it. We let the typical cuts, bumps, bruises, swollen thumbs from hitting them with a hammer, sweat and discouragement simply happen because it was life. These issues were temporary, not life-altering, and the kids needed to learn it. They needed to learn to persevere when they didn't feel like it. So did I. We weren't tyrants and never gave tasks beyond each child's capacity, but we definitely let life stretch them, and we would not trade those years for anything.

I encourage you to allow "safe" adversity to visit your children, and let them learn through it, without a premature life preserver. Simply add your strength to theirs when and where they need it and watch them blossom.

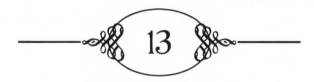

Repentance

When our first two were born, Justin and Bear, our oldest sons, I really wasn't a very good dad. I still had too many fig leaves in my spiritual closet, so I was dealing with that baggage while learning to guide a family in Christ's love. In hindsight, I now realize the key factor back then was not how well I did, but rather what I did about what I was not doing right. In other words, like many parents, we practice out our insecurities and shortcomings on our oldest and then get into a rhythm of parenting. The problem was that it was at the expense of my oldest boys. Consequently, as I was missing the mark, I essentially repented my way through much of their early years. This also includes Lindsay Ruth, my oldest daughter, but she was so easy to raise that my "stuff" didn't affect her as much. The boys and I have discussed this over the years, and they both communicated to me the importance of me humbling myself to them when I blew it. Again, I give credit to Vernice Smith, my spiritual father, who emphasized the cross-filled life in all that we do.

This repentance was as important, as a young husband and father still at war with himself at the time, as it was to guide my sons beside still waters. Yet this was a challenge when I defaulted into old fig leaf patterns and caused unease in the souls of my boys as I was inaccurately representing Jesus to them. The remedy was not complicated. I repented my way through their earliest years, and as a result, the Lord kept their young consciences free of guilt and self-condemnation. We were able to keep the air between us clear.

My approach, by God's grace, was straightforward. When I blew it with impatience, yelling, or intolerance, I'd ask them to forgive me in the following way: "Son, Dad has sinned against the Lord and against you. I had no right to treat you like that, even if you disobeyed. I am here to show you the love of Jesus, and I blew it, so will you forgive me for [name the sin here]?"

I'd wait, and they always graciously forgave. Then I asked them to pray with me to "help Dad get right with Jesus so I could be a better dad." I was thus giving them covenantal power to forgive me, and be restored to a place of respect in their souls. There was a mutual reconciling of our consciences and renewal to right relationship in Christ. I did the same with my girls, but they didn't push my buttons the way the boys could.

Vernice had drilled into me to not defend myself either when falsely accused or when I was wrong. If wrong, just admit it, repent, get cleansing for all parties involved, and move on with gratitude. It's really counterintuitive to our human nature as we want to defend, protect our reputation, and always present ourselves in the best light. Yet humility unto repentance opens the hearts of all involved, removes any insecure posturing, and opens the door for honest relationships. For example, about seven or eight years ago, I went to my son Bear and asked him to forgive me for anything I had done over the years that I had not made right. He told me that it gave him a deeper spiritual release in his own soul in ways different than previously.

The Lord's plan is amazingly effective. When I surrender my right to be right, He gives grace to the humbling of myself, releases me from false burdens to make things happen, to change people, and restores what needs restoring, while bringing about His plan that I prayed for in the first place. Pure genius!

Sadly, over the years, many young men have told me that their Christian dads have seldom, if ever, repented for sins against the family. I'm not even talking about the insufficient "I'm sorry" apology; rather the dad releasing the power of the covenant upon their children and wives through the practice of repentance unto renewal.

His grace is more than abundant for you to begin right now if you need to. If you're unsure, ask your wife or older children if you have sinned against them and give them liberty to be honest. The fruit in all of you, including your unborn descendants, is more than worth it.

Thinking Like a Gatekeeper

In the hundreds of weddings I've officiated over the decades, never once did I walk out first with the bride and watch the groom walk up the aisle to be "given away" by dad to his new wife.

This leads us to our final challenge: think like the man in the gate at all times. Then, you will act like it. The key, friends, is rather straightforward. Become an initiator in life, first, in your walk with Jesus, then your family, and finally in the culture around you. This means embracing the previous sections covered in part II in a proactive way and putting them into practice. Of course, this requires us to "initiate" the process so that it will happen.

The good news is that as gatekeepers, the Lord has put it in our souls to be covenant initiators and not just receptors in life. We pursue the girl, we protect, provide and guide, and these are no passive actions.

Jesus is the ultimate initiator, from Adam to Abraham to David to the cross. He continually invaded life with His redemptive plan in each man's life and preserved them in the journey. Now that His work on Earth is finished, the life of the Covenant Initiator is imputed to all men who put their trust in Jesus alone for salvation, as His Holy Spirit dwells within us. Thus, we can do it, if we seek Him first, submit, obey, and renew when we mess up. We must activate our awareness meter, understand depravity, confront our passivity, clear the conscience, and live a repentant life. The goal and motive is to live redemptively toward all lives we touch, edifying and influencing them in greater ways than before they spent time with us.

Perhaps the most incredible example of thinking as a gatekeeper comes from the Lord Jesus as He is suffering on the cross as no one has ever suffered. John recorded a moment between him; Jesus; and Mary, the Lord's mother, in John 19:26–27.

> When Jesus saw his mother and the disciple whom he loved standing nearby, he said to his mother, "Woman, behold your son!" Then he said to his disciple, "Behold your mother!" And from that hour the disciple took her to his own home.

John is referring to himself as "the disciple whom Jesus loved" since he was his best friend, so we have a direct and eyewitness account of Jesus performing His covenant duties of the firstborn to ensure the care of his surviving mother (Mary was a widow at this time).

Every time I read this, I'm amazed and ask myself the same question: "Why did Jesus wait until His gruesome and atoning death moment to commission John to care for His mother?" It's hard to imagine the Son of Man carrying the wisdom of heaven, not having spoken with John about this beforehand as they were best friends, and John recorded how thorough Jesus's final teaching was at the Last Supper in chapters 14 to 17.

Jesus was the ultimate steward, so although it's not recorded, my money is on Jesus having already not only approached this with John and Mary but discussed the plan as well. Remember, Jesus had half brothers who served Him, yet He chose John. Thus, some preliminary preparation of the family had to have happened to allow this incredible moment to happen.

Jesus only spoke seven sayings while on the cross, and this was one of them! Why? Well, He was modeling the ultimate example of a gatekeeper covering his family, and if He did this while on the cross, do you think it might be really important?! This amazing example motivated me and Sandra to bring our aging parents into our home and live with us and to care for them as they aged. Not always easy but a privilege, now we see the impact it had on our eight children to think generationally like Jesus did on the cross. What a gift from Him! Thank you, Lord.

So, my friend, the path has been laid out before us as men. Our first calling from God is to keep the gate in our families through good times and trials. As we do, His mercies greet us every morning to be it and do it as imperfect as we are. I encourage you to go for it in His name.

May the Holy Spirit, the Covenant Initiator, invade us so we can invade life around us, starting with our families. Amen.

Some Highly Recommended Books

There are thousands of books out there, but I'm only suggesting a few that have had a great impact on me in my journey as a gatekeeper from cluelessness to today. May they guide and impact you as they have done to me, and continue to do so.

1. The Holiness of God *by R.C. Sproul.* Dr. Sproul brilliantly paints a picture of who this Most High God really is. It drives me to my knees in both worship and the fear of the Lord. A must for a gatekeeper's soul. I reread it regularly.

2. A Tale of Three Kings *by Gene Edwards.* A most unusual but gripping read about the beauty of brokenness before God and man. Every gatekeeper must be broken to be entrusted by God with the power to keep the gate.

3. Essential Truths of the Christian Faith *by R. C. Sproul.* Again, the late great R. C. Sproul is the man. This is a clear and concise summary of the doctrines of the Christian faith, each one written in Dr. Sproul's so easy-to-understand style and with amazing brevity for guys who don't want a long read. I consider this an absolute must as a reference tool for a gatekeeper so he may know what he believes, and why he believes it. You'll be able to guide your children into solid theological understanding, even when they're young, and prepare them for launch.

4. What the Bible Says About Child Training *by J. Richard Fugate.* Sandra and I read this as we began our family, and it nailed it for us both. The author relentlessly sticks to the Holy Scriptures to clearly explain the why and how of discipline and training that God intended parents to apply.

He makes no appeals to other schools of thought and thus provides the gatekeeper with a valuable and practical go-to tool for every child, even the tough ones. God's wisdom and instruction are clear.

About the Author

Dr. Jerry Tallo was raised in Upstate New York in a tough Italian Catholic family with parents who paid a price for their three sons. Converted to Christ in 1979, he met Sandra in 1980, and they married that year. They had eight children, who by God's grace all serve Jesus, and are blessed with seventeen grandchildren (so far). To them, family is wealth.

From the outset, Jerry and Sandy carried a generational worldview in which all the generations serve one another in healthy community, where men, women, and young adults are equipped to be influencers in society by fulfilling God given destinies.

Jerry served as a lead pastor for about three decades. Since 2016 he now mentors young pastors in two states, to make them successful in their families and ministries.

His passion to see men restored to their God-created image fuels him daily.

Sandy has a BS in music, and Jerry a PhD in church history.

Jerry and Sandy's ministry is called "Anchored"
You can find many of Jerry's teachings, articles and
resources at their website: www.anchoredministry.com.

CPSIA information can be obtained
at www.ICGtesting.com
Printed in the USA
BVHW081024210622
640287BV00005B/160